PICTORIAL HISTORY OF THE
DEMOCRATIC
PARTY

PICTORIAL HISTORY OF THE
DEMOCRATIC PARTY

By Beryl Frank

CASTLE BOOKS

A Division of
BOOK SALES, INC.
110 Enterprise Avenue
Secaucus, N.J. 07094

ISBN: 0-89009-337-7
Library of Congress Catalog Card Number: 79-92978

Acknowledgments

The search for the pictorial history of the Democratic Party began at the National Museum of History and Technology, Smithsonian Institution.

All of the photographs included here comes from the files of the Smithsonian Institution.

The author wishes to acknowledge those pictures that came from the private collections of James Barnes and Kenton Broyles as well as photographs taken from the Ralph E. Becker Collection at the Smithsonian Institution.

Special thanks are offered to Mr. Herbert R. Collins, Curator, Division of Political History, Smithsonian Institution, for his assistance with this project and for writing the Special Introduction to this book.

Thanks also to the unsung heroes and heroines of the many libraries, who unfailingly answered questions of a technical nature with smiles on their faces. And most of all, thanks to Lou, who knows who he is and always understands.

Contents

Introduction

The history of the Democratic Party really includes the history of every town and city where a voter has cast his or her ballot in a national, state, or local election. However, to be complete, such a history would fill volumes.

This pictorial history of the Democratic Party covers every presidential election in which a Democrat was a candidate. You will find dates and places where the Democratic Party has been important nationally. Primarily, this history will deal with the national presidential elections, which for the most part reflect the Democratic ideologies that have come down to the present day.

The Democratic Party held its first national convention in May, 1832, in Baltimore, Maryland. To some attending the convention, the party was still known as the Democratic-Republicans, because its roots went back to the Republicanism of Thomas Jefferson. But the party, which renominated Andrew Jackson for president in 1832, dropped the word Republican from its name at that time—and the Democratic Party was born.

The history of the party, therefore, begins in 1832. The Democrats have nominated presidential candidates in every national election since that date. While the Democratic candidates have not always won, the party has been a major force in the American political system for more than 150 years.

Special Introduction

When Americans go to the polls to cast their votes for an individual they are also voting for ideas and principals which have been carefully structured from a chaotic scene into a cohesive organization known as a party. For a nation of people to cast their votes without such a political mechanism would be void of order, direction or purpose. Few probably realize that, when the Constitution of the United States was written, no provisions were made for political parties. There are no provisions for nominating conventions, caucuses, party committees or chairmen, nor indeed for other details of party machinery. One cannot conclude, however, that by their absence the founding fathers did not anticipate such elements in the system.

In the beginning of our republic, no one thought much about political parties—George Washington, our first president, was elected unanimously. Also, only a small element of our society was permitted to vote. By the time of the election of 1800, we did have a two-party system, but no mechanism to prevent electing a President and Vice-President from opposing parties and platforms. Since that time, America has mostly maintained a two-party system. It is probably a tradition we inherited from our English forebearers where comparable conflicts arose between the Tory and Whig factions. It is certainly unlike the system used in France and most of the European countries.

Party organization has had a long evolution, deriving from social needs, government structure and expansion of franchise. Party platforms became more complicated as reform movements were pressured by splinter parties, many of which dissolved or merged with other parties when their platforms were adopted by major parties. No longer did voter privileges rest in the hands of men whose social position and character or money placed them in the natural ascendancy of position or leadership. As the forces in the American experience shifted, so did the political parties in principal and name.

It is difficult to define a particular party. Since the Civil War, the Democratic Party has depended on the North-South coalition supported by rural agricultural interests in the South and the urban proletariat in the North. However, logical as this appears, the truth of the matter is that, at some time, both major parties have been on all sides of most of the issues. In fact the Democrats have been very dependent on the support of the western farmers since 1932.

The Democratic Party of the 20th century has it origins in the Republican Party of Jefferson and the Democratic Party of Jackson. To add to the confusion of the name, the two merged as the Democratic-Republican Party before the name finally changed again to the Democratic Party.

Although the standard symbol for the party, the donkey, did not evolve until the 1870s, the portraits and names of Jefferson and Jackson were identified early with the party. Other symbols, including the rooster, have also been identified with the Democratic Party.

This pictorial study reflects the party's changing aspirations and the various campaign paraphernalia employed to nominate a candidate to the party and elect him to office. The political ideals are visually evident throughout and will most certainly stimulate the reader to explore other writings concerning the origin and history of the Democratic Party.

Herbert R. Collins

President: **Democrats**
Andrew Jackson*

Vice–President: **Martin Van Buren**

National Republicans
Henry Clay
John Sergeant

Ralph E. Becker Collection

During Andrew Jackson's first term in office, prior to the first Democratic National Convention, the President surrounded himself with some trusted friends who were not well known in Washington circles. This group of advisors was commonly called Jackson's Kitchen Cabinet. By 1831 the Kitchen Cabinet had lost most of its influence, and by 1832 an unknown cartoonist was showing Mr. Jackson cleaning out his cabinet in favor of other advisors.

*Winning candidates will be shown in blue for every election throughout the book. Only the majority losing candidates will be listed.

John C. Calhoun, who was vice-president during Jackson's first term of office, was one of the political rats leaving Jackson's "Falling House." The cabinet resigned due to Jackson's interference in a social matter. Peggy Eaton, wife of Jackson's secretary of war, was not considered socially acceptable and was snubbed by other cabinet wives. The President interceded on her behalf and this caused the mass resignation. The third rat from the left was Martin Van Buren, whose tail was held fast by the President's foot.

While this cartoon was directed at Andrew Jackson's veto of the rechartering of the United States Bank—a veto that was popular with the common man of that day—it is perhaps more noteworthy that Jackson was riding on a donkey. This was the first cartoon to show a Democrat represented by a donkey, which was not yet the official party symbol.

The issue of rechartering the United States Bank was one that the Whig Party wanted to use against Andrew Jackson in his bid for reelection. However, Jackson's veto of the bank bill only endeared him further to the populace.

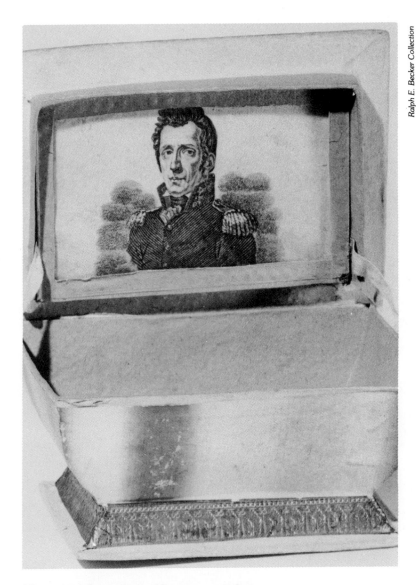

The sewing box pictured here was made in France for the political campaign of Andrew Jackson, whose portrait is shown on the inside lid. Similar boxes were also produced for Jackson's opponent, John Quincy Adams.

The Cry of Imperialism is Not New—The following is a fac-simile reproduction of a famous caricature used against Andrew Jackson, in the campaign of 1832, when he sought and secured re-election.

BORN TO COMMAND.

OF VETO MEMORY.

HAD I BEEN CONSULTED.

KING ANDREW THE FIRST.

KING ANDREW

THE FIRST,

" *Born to Command.*"

A **KING** who, possessing as much power as his *Gracious Brother William IV.*, makes a worse use of it.

A **KING** who has placed himself above the laws, as he has shown by his contempt of our judges.

A **KING** who would destroy our currency, and substitute *Old Rags*, payable by no one knows who, and no one knows where, instead of *good Silver Dollars*.

A **KING** born to command, as he has shown himself by appointing men to office contrary to the will of the people.

A **KING** who, while he was feeding his favourites out of the public money, denied a pittance to the *Old Soldiers* who fought and bled for our independence.

A **KING** whose *Prime Minister* and *Heir Apparent*, was thought unfit for the office of ambassador by the people:

Shall he reign over us,

Or shall the PEOPLE RULE?

This was a famous caricature of Andrew Jackson in the campaign of 1832. It was reproduced in 1900 for use on a political poster.

1836

President:
Vice-President:

Democrats
Martin Van Buren
Richard M. Johnson

Whigs
William Henry Harrison
Francis Granger

Much of what is shown in this cartoon occurred during the years of Jackson's presidency, from 1832 until 1836. However, the cartoon was probably drawn just prior to the election of 1836 in opposition to Martin Van Buren. The last square in the cartoon depicts General William Henry Harrison of Ohio, the opposition candidate, crowing as winner. Contrary to this cartoon Van Buren, the Democratic candidate, won the election.

Martin Van Buren, the son of a tavern keeper and a native of New York, had served as vice-president under Andrew Jackson. His appearance was so meticulous that his opposition accused him of using cologne water and lacing his figure in with corsets. These charges could have been quite damaging to the candidate in a time when the rough-and-ready man was most popular.

This colorful Martin Van Buren campaign banner sported the patriotic colors of red, white, and blue. The center field is cherry red with white letters, and the national eagle is also in white. The border stripes are blue as are the stars in the white stripe. By 1836 street banners had become standard campaign paraphernalia.

The issue of whether to use hard money rather than paper money to pay for public lands was known as Specie, and Van Buren continued his predecessor's policy for Specie. This small jewelry pin saying "O.K. Specie" may have been worn proudly by one of Van Buren's female supporters.

BEFORE AND AFTER
A LOCOFOCO CHRISTMAS·PRESENT·

A LOCOFOCO

before the N.York election

Designed & published by D.C. Johnston. 6 Summer St.
BOSTON

The Locofoco group was an offshoot of the 1836 Democratic National Convention, which was held in New York City. When the meeting was formally adjourned and the gas lights were turned out, members of this group lit the then-new friction matches called "locofocos," thus giving the group its name. The Locofocos, which became a third but minor party, opposed Martin Van Buren and crusaded for labor and equal rights. With their strong opposition to the banks and "paper capitalism," the Locofocos became a minor thorn in the side of the Democratic Party.

The medal shown here with a picture of Van Buren on one side reads "Democracy and our country" on its reverse side. Such medals were carried as lucky pocket tokens by the men or worn around the neck by the ladies. This is the ancestor of today's campaign button.

ELECTORAL TICKET.

FOR PRESIDENT,
MARTIN VAN BUREN.
FOR VICE PRESIDENT,
RICHARD M. JOHNSON.

1st District.—*ARTHUR SMITH*, of Isle of Wight.

2d District.—*JOHN CARGILL*, of Sussex.

3d District.—*JAMES JONES*, of Nottoway.

4th District.—*WM. R. BASKERVILLE*, of Mecklenburg.

5th District.—*CHARLES YANCEY*, of Buckingham.

6th District.—*RICHARD LOGAN*, of Halifax.

7th District.—*ARCHIBALD STUART*, of Patrick.

8th District.—*WILLIAM JONES*, of Gloucester.

9th District.—*AUSTIN BROCKENBROUGH*, of Essex.

10th District.—*JOHN GIBSON*, of Prince William.

11th District.—*J. D HALYBURTON*, of New Kent.

12th District.—*THOMAS J. RANDOLPH*, of Albemarle.

13th District.—*WALLER HOLLADAY*, of Spottsylvania.

14th District.—*INMAN HORNER*, of Fauquier.

15th District.— *James Gibson of Hampshire*

16th District.— *WILLIAM A. HARRIS*, of Page.

17th District.—*JACOB D. WILLIAMSON*, of Rockingham

18th District.—*WILLIAM TAYLOR*, of Rockbridge.

19th District.—*AUGUSTUS A. CHAPMAN*, of Monroe.

20th District.—*JAMES HOGE*, of Pulaski.

21st District.— *WILLIAM BYARS*, of Washington.

22d District.—*BENJAMIN BROWN*, of Cabell.

23d District.—*JOHN HINDMAN*, of Brooke.

This electoral ticket, used in Virginia in 1836, is typical of what the voters used at that time. Votes were folded and placed in wooden ballot boxes at many voting polls. Note the hand-written addition of a candidate's name—probably added to the ticket when a candidate dropped out after the ticket was printed.

President: Democrats **Martin Van Buren** Whigs **William Henry Harrison**
Vice-President: **Richard M. Johnson** **John Tyler**

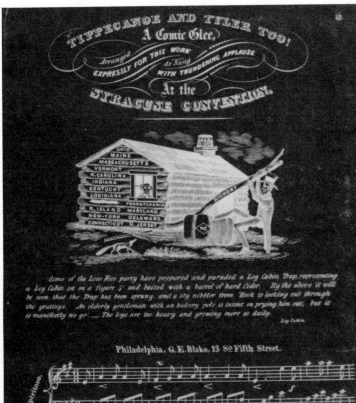

Martin Van Buren, the New York aristocrat, is wistfully looking out the window of his opposition's log cabin while the old man Andrew Jackson attempts to pry him out. A correspondent to a Baltimore newspaper had suggested if "Old Tip," as Van Buren was called, were given money and a barrel of hard cider, he would prefer a log cabin to the White House. This comment, aimed to gain Democratic votes, provided the Whig opposition with their winning campaign slogan, "log cabin and hard cider."

The simple soldier-farmer Harrison was quite a contrast to the aristocratic Democratic candidate. The hard cider being distributed by the Whigs from campaign wagons like the one shown here helped send Van Buren back to his own home town instead of to the White House.

William Henry Harrison is pictured here on a quilt made of his own campaign and inaugural ribbons. He survived his inauguration by just one month and died on April 4, 1841.

John Tyler, elected vice-president in 1840, was sworn into office as president shortly after Harrison's death. Tyler became the tenth president of the United States.

	Democrats	Whigs
President:	James K. Polk	Henry Clay
Vice-President:	George M. Dallas	Theodore Frelinghuysen

James K. Polk of Tennessee was the first dark horse presidential candidate. He was not well known nationally, and it shocked the political experts when he won the needed convention votes in Baltimore on May 27, 1844. The vice-presidential candidate, George M. Dallas of Pennsylvania, won the nomination despite strong feelings in the party for Van Buren.

The cock overcoming the coon shown on this campaign ribbon were the party symbols of the day. It was up to a later cartoonist by the name of Thomas Nast to create the symbols used today to represent the Democrats and the Republicans—the donkey and the elephant.

This Democratic national badge featured the important issue of the re-annexation of Texas. Henry Clay, the Whig candidate, was opposed to this major issue. However, the theme of "union, harmony, and vigilance" was to win the day for the Democrats.

The re-occupation of Oregon was also a major issue in the campaign of 1844. The West was growing and Americans wanted to own their own land. Polk won the election with his support of expansionism.

	Democrats	Whigs
President:	Lewis Cass	Zachary Taylor
Vice-President:	William O. Butler	Millard Fillmore

Senator Lewis Cass of Michigan, a New Englander by birth but a westerner by choice, was the cautious elder statesman who carried the Democratic banner in the 1848 election. His running mate was William O. Butler of Kentucky. Note the eagle shown at the top of this Democratic banner huddled over a world comprised of America and France.

ZACHARY TAYLOR,
PEOPLE'S CANDIDATE FOR PRESIDENT.

MILLARD FILLMORE,
WHIG CANDIDATE FOR VICE PRESIDENT.

The Democratic opposition in 1848 was the popular "Rough-and-Ready" Zachary Taylor and his running mate, Millard Fillmore.

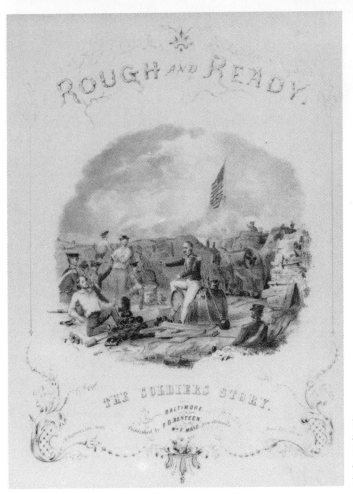

General Zachary Taylor was Lewis Cass' formidable opponent. Sheet music of the day stressed the general's military career. Sheet music has always been used by candidates for presidential office, because it is a good, emotional way of stirring the voters.

Ralph E. Becker Collection

The question asked by the man on the left in this cartoon from 1848 sums up the Democrats' feelings about Zachary Taylor: "What for a President would he make?" No one could forsee, least of all the cartoonist, that President Zachary Taylor would die only sixteen months after taking office and be succeeded at that time by his vice president, Millard Fillmore.

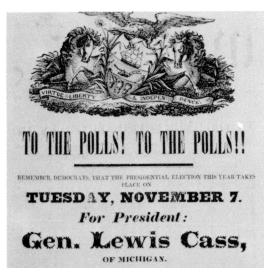

The issue of Irish immigration was an important factor for eastern voters in the campaign of 1848. The American Irish contingent sympathized with the men of old Erin, but they had adopted the United States as their home. However, some wanted the country to open its doors to the suffering Irish who were on the brink of the potato famine. Patrick O'Connell, shown in the cartoon on Ireland's shores, was declaring himself against slavery in that country. While immigration was not considered a major issue, it was evidence that the United States was affected by events that happened across the ocean.

This 1848 Democratic ballot broadside stressed the importance of getting out the vote. The small print tells the Democrats of Lancaster County to be careful, to count the votes, and to preserve the ballot boxes. It reads in part, "We have the majority of the state and need only bring the full Democratic vote to the Polls to secure the state for Cass and Butler . . ." However, that state's vote for the Democratic candidates was not enough to win the presidency that year throughout the nation.

29

	Democrats	Whigs
President:	Franklin Pierce	Winfield Scott
Vice-President:	William R. King	William A. Graham

Although people did not know dark horse Democratic candidate Franklin Pierce of New Hampshire very well, he was forty-seven years old, a good temperance man, and a fluent speaker with few party enemies. His victory over Winfield Scott was the largest electoral victory since that of James Monroe, before the Democratic Party was born. Note that the cock or rooster was still used to symbolize the Democratic Party.

General Pierce, whose Mexican War record was brave but not brilliant, is shown on this campaign handkerchief as a future president. The names and dates of all the former presidents appear in the leafed border.

Pennant medallions were standard campaign material in the middle-nineteenth-century. This one shows the good-looking Franklin Pierce, who seemed to please all of the party members. Pierce was able to unite the party and lead it on to victory.

This lithograph by George Caleb Bingham portrays the kind of campaigning done at this point in history. The method of campaigning shown was known as "Stump Speaking." The speaker was slightly raised above the crowd, probably on a stump, and the gathered people listened intently to form their own opinions of what the speaker had to say.

This lithograph by John Sartain is titled "The County Election." Note the sign, which reads, "The will of the people, the supreme law." This sign seems to apply only to the men. There were no women present or voting in a county election in that era.

	Democrats	Republicans	American Know-Nothings
President:	James Buchanan	John C. Fremont	Millard Fillmore
Vice-President:	John C. Breckinridge	William L. Dayton	Andrew J. Donelson

Party principles were written out on this presidential campaign ballot. They read: "The Constitution, the Sovereignty and equality of the States; The Repeal of the Missouri Restriction; The people of the Territories in forming State Governments to adopt their own institutions." However, it was probably not these principles alone that won the election for Mr. Buchanan. The Republicans and the Know-Nothings, so called because they answered "I know nothing" to all questions, were both offshoots of the old Whigs. It was this split in the Whig party that ultimately threw the election of 1856 to the Democrats.

James Buchanan of Pennsylvania had served as Minister to England and managed to escape taking definite stands on such party-splitting issues as compromise in the territories. By this means, he was acceptable to the South as well as the North. His running mate, John C. Breckinridge, was from Kentucky.

"Ten cent Jimmy" was likened to a donkey in this anti-Buchanan cartoon. Despite opposition of this kind even within the Democratic Party, he won the party nomination over Stephen Douglas and Franklin Pierce, whose stand on slavery was not acceptable to the party at large.

This James Buchanan medal, showing the candidate's likeness, also showed one of his policies—that of no sectionalism. With over forty years of experience in politics and three previous attempts at the presidency, Buchanan entered the White House as an experienced statesman but a colorless, conservative figure.

	Democrats	Republicans	Southern Democrats
President:	Stephen A. Douglas	Abraham Lincoln	John C. Breckinridge
Vice-President:	Herschel V. Johnson	Hannibal Hamlin	Joseph Lane

"The Little Giant," Senator Stephen A. Douglas, gained national fame in his victorious senatorial debates with Abraham Lincoln in 1858. In 1860 a bitter but unsuccessful Democratic convention in Charleston, South Carolina, forced the party to convene again in Baltimore. Senator Douglas won the nomination for the presidency. The "Schottisch" sheet music shown here became a campaign message for Douglas.

The Democratic southern seceders convened in Richmond, Va., on June 11, 1860, and nominated their own slate, which included John C. Breckinridge of Kentucky and Joseph Lane of Oregon.

REPUBLICAN UNION TICKET

FOR GOVERNOR,
WILLIAM A. BUCKINGHAM.
FOR LIEUT. GOVERNOR,
ROGER AVERILL.
FOR SECRETARY,
J. HAMMOND TRUMBULL.
FOR TREASURER,
GABRIEL W. COITE.
FOR COMPTROLLER,
LEMAN W. CUTLER.
FOR CONGRESS,
HENRY C. DEMING.
FOR SENATOR,
LUCIUS S. FULLER.
FOR SHERIFF,
AMOS PEASE.
JUDGE OF PROBATE,
CALEB HOPKINS.

PROHIBITION TICKET

"IN GOD WE TRUST."

FOR GOVERNOR,
JOSEPH CUMMINGS.
FOR LIEUTENANT-GOVERNOR,
GEORGE P. ROGERS.
FOR SECRETARY OF STATE,
RUEL P. COWLES.
FOR TREASURER,
JOHN A. ROCKWELL.
FOR COMPTROLLER,
MARVIN A. DEAN.
FOR MEMBER OF CONGRESS,
ELIAS B. HILLARD.
FOR SENATOR 17th District,
WILLIAM E. PETTEE.
FOR JUDGE OF PROBATE.

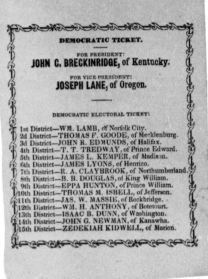

DEMOCRATIC TICKET.

FOR PRESIDENT:
JOHN C. BRECKINRIDGE, of Kentucky,
FOR VICE PRESIDENT:
JOSEPH LANE, of Oregon.

DEMOCRATIC ELECTORAL TICKET:

1st District—WM. LAMB, of Norfolk City.
2d District—THOMAS F. GOODE, of Mecklenburg.
3d District—JOHN R. EDMUNDS, of Halifax.
4th District—T. T. TREDWAY, of Prince Edward.
5th District—JAMES L. KEMPER, of Madison.
6th District—JAMES LYONS, of Henrico.
7th District—R. A. CLAYBROOK, of Northumberland.
8th District—B. B. DOUGLAS, of King William.
9th District—EPPA HUNTON, of Prince William.
10th District—THOMAS M. ISBELL, of Jefferson.
11th District—JAS. W. MASSIE, of Rockbridge.
12th District—WM. H. ANTHONY, of Botetourt.
13th District—ISAAC B. DUNN, of Washington.
14th District—JOHN G. NEWMAN, of Kanawha.
15th District—ZEDEKIAH KIDWELL, of Marion.

WHIG TICKET.

FOR GOVERNOR,
EMORY WASHBURN,
OF WORCESTER.

FOR LIEUT. GOVERNOR,
WILLIAM C. PLUNKETT,
OF ADAMS.

FOR SENATORS,
GEO. HOWLAND, Jr., of New Bedford,
WILLARD BLACKINTON, of Attleboro',
RICHARD BORDEN, of Fall River.

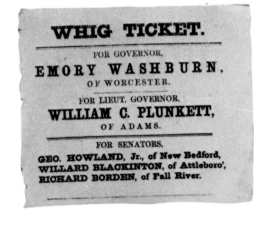

The Democratic ticket shown here was for the Southern Democrats, who pulled away from the main party and nominated John C. Breckinridge as their candidate. This major split in the Democratic Party is considered by many to have been what placed Republican Abraham Lincoln in the White House.

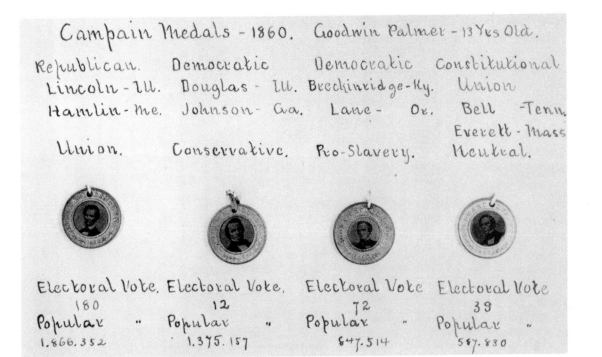

These campaign medals were saved by a thirteen-year-old boy named Goodwin Palmer. His hand-written statistics show the results of the election of 1860.

This tongue-in-cheek cartoon shows the difficulties Stephen Douglas faced because of his own party's opposition candidate, John Breckinridge.

Abraham Lincoln climbs here to the presidency despite both Stephen Douglas and John C. Breckinridge. These two Democrats are shown as small figures sparring with each other in boxing gloves. Even the minor Constitutional Union Party's candidate, Bell of Tennessee, is shown in this cartoon.

This slavery print, probably drawn about 1860, contrasts American slaves with English slaves. According to the pro-slavery cartoonist, American slaves were much better off than their English counterparts. This was an incendiary cartoon in a country that was split over the issue of slavery.

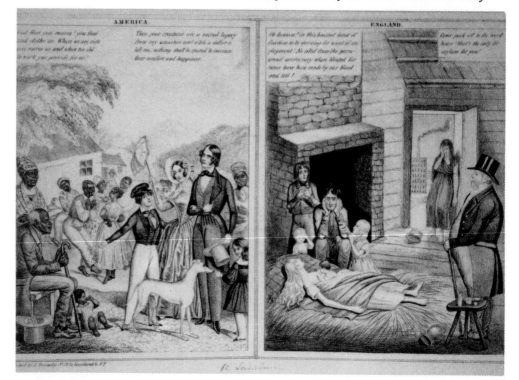

	Democrats	Republicans
President:	George B. McClellan	Abraham Lincoln
Vice-President:	George H. Pendleton	Andrew Johnson

Despite General McClellan's removal from the military in 1862, he remained popular with the soldiers of the Army of the Potomac. His grievances with the Republican administration, and his blaming the administration for the current military failures, gave him the Democratic nomination for president in 1864.

The Democratic convention was held in Chicago in August, 1864, and featured a war hero candidate and a strong peace platform. Enthusiastic Democrats came to this convention on foot and by horse-and-carriage, as well as on horseback.

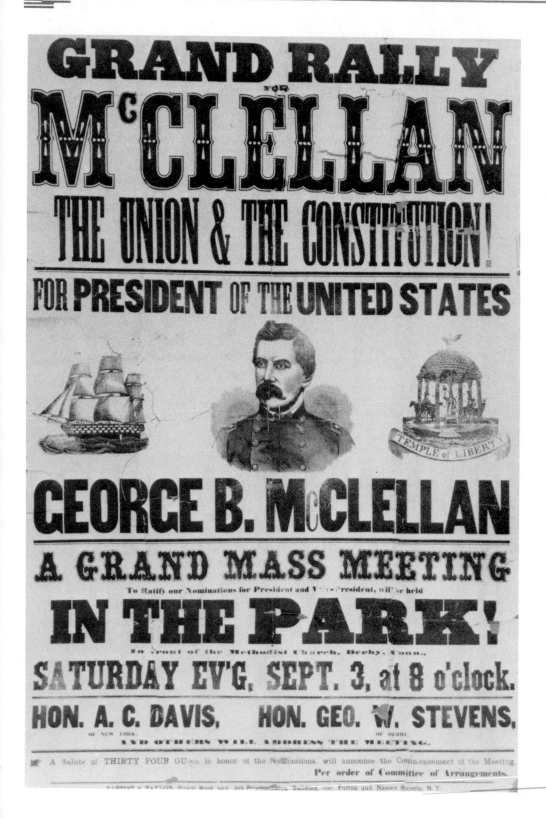

This broadside was posted prominently to rally party members to the side of General McClellan. The slogan — "The Union and the Constitution" — was a popular cry heard wherever Democrats assembled.

Campaign bandannas of the day, like the one shown here, featured pictures of prominent Democrats throughout the land. Many military figures were shown here and, of course, General McClellan was featured in the center of the handkerchief. The sheathed sword, and the gun and cannon that weren't able to be fired, showed the party emphasis on what the country longed for — peace and unity.

By 1864 the torchlight procession was a favorite kind of campaign rally. This one took place in New York as the Democrats electioneered for their presidential candidate, McClellan.

The lantern, which has General McClellan's picture on one side and the slogan "Union and the Constitution" on the other side was carried in the torchlight parades.

LITTLE MACK & HIS PARTY „GOING UP" SALT RIVER ON A GUN BOAT,
Terrific Explosion of the „Quaker Gun" and destruction of the entire party.

The lack of harmony in the Democratic Party is shown clearly in this cartoon. There were members in favor of restoration of the Union, and "War Democrats" who wanted total victory against the South. Jefferson Davis is shown sinking here; McClellan and other prominent Democrats of the day are being destroyed. Lincoln stands in the background holding onto the Emancipation Proclamation. The Salt River was the river with no ending — a purely political term used in the last half of the nineteenth century.

This anti-McClellan cartoon refers to his wartime service under Lincoln, which was considered unsatisfactory and caused his removal from the military. The nation is saying to McClellan: "You shall rise no more to any position to do me harm, — you shall dig your own grave and be forgotten forever."

LITTLE MAC TRYING TO DIG HIS WAY TO THE WHITE HOUSE BUT IS FRIGHTENED BY SPIRITUAL MANIFESTATIONS.—

Still another anti-McClellan cartoon shows McClellan restoring slavery to the South, while Lincoln is shown requiring unconditional submission to the government. This was a touchy and emotional issue in both the Union and the Confederacy.

Here, McClellan and Lincoln debate the issue of what to do with the country, which was still at war. Lincoln states here — "I think it best to give the old bull dog full swing to go in and finish them." "Little Mac" was weakly upholding the peace platform of his party.

LATEST.

Death of the President.

WAR DEPARTMENT,
Washington, April 15th, 8 P. M.

To Major General Dix:

Abraham Lincoln died this morning at twenty-two minutes after 7 o'clock.

E. M. STANTON, Secretary of War.

WASHINGTON, APRIL 15, 11 O'CLOCK A. M.— The Star extra says:—

"At twenty minutes past seven o'clock the President breathed his last, closing his eyes as if falling to sleep, and his countenance assuming an expression of perfect serenity. There were no indications of pain, and it was not known that he was dead until the gradual decreasing respiration ceased altogether.

The Rev. Dr Gurley, of the New York Avenue Presbyterian Church, immediately on its being ascertained that life was extinct, knelt at the bedside and offered an impressive prayer, which was responded to by all present.

Dr Gurley then proceeded to the front parlor, where Mrs Lincoln, Captain Robert Lincoln, Mr John Hay, the private secretary, and other were waiting, where he again offered a prayer for the consolation of the family.

The following minutes, taken by Dr Abbott, show the condition of the late President throughout the night:—

11.00 o'clock	Pulse 44.	
11.05 do	do 45,	and growing weaker.
11.10 do	do 45.	
11.15 do	do 42.	
11.20 do	do 45;	respiration 27 to 29.
11.25 do	do 42	
11.32 do	do 48,	and full.
11.40 do	do 45.	
11.45 do	do 45;	respiration 22.
12.00 do	do 48;	respiration 22.
12.15 do	do 48;	respiration 21; ecchymosis in both eyes.
12.20 do	do 45.	
12.32 do	do 60.	
12.35 do	do 66.	
12.40 do	do 69;	right eye much swollen and ecchymosis.
12.45 do	do 70.	
12.55 do	do 80;	struggling motion of arms.
1.00 do	do 86;	respiration 30.
1.30 do	do 95;	appearing easier.
1.45 do	do 86;	very quiet; respiration irregular; Mrs Lincoln present.
2.10 do		Mrs Lincoln retired with Robert Lincoln to an adjoining room.
2.30 do		President very quiet; pulse 54; respiration 28.
2.52 do		Pulse 48; respiration 30.
3.00 do		Visited again by Mrs Lincoln.
3.25 do		Respiration 24, and regular.
3.35 do		Prayer by Rev. Dr Gurley.
4.00 do		Respiration 26, and regular.
4.15 do		Pulse 60; respiration 25.
5.50 do		Respiration 28; regular; sleeping.
6.00 do		Pulse failing; respiration 28.
6.30 do		Still failing, and labored breathing.
7.00 do		Symptoms of immediate dissolution.
7.22 do		DEATH.

Surrounding the deathbed of the President, were Secretaries Stanton, Welles, Usher, Attorney-General Speed, Postmaster-General Dennison, M. B. Field, Assistant Secretary of the Treasury, Judge Otto, Assistant Secretary of the Interior, General Halleck, General Meigs, Senator Sumner, R. F. Andrews, of New York; General Todd, of Dacotah; John Hay, private Secretary; Governor Oglesby, of Illinois; General Farnsworth, Mrs and Miss Kenney, Miss Harris, Captain Robert Lincoln, son of the President, and Doctors E. W. Abbott, R. K. Stone, C. D. Gatch, Neal Hall, and Mr Lieberman. Secretary McCulloch remained with the President until about 5 o'clock and Chief Justice Chase after several hours' attendance during the night, returned early this morning.

Immediately after the President's death a Cabinet meeting was called by Secretary Stanton, and held in the room in which the corpse lay. Secretaries Stanton, Welles and Usher, Postmaster-General Dennison and Attorney-General Speed were present.

SECOND DESPATCH·

WASHINGTON, APRIL 15.—The President's body was removed from the private residence opposite Ford's Theatre to the Executive Mansion this morning, at half-past nine o'clock, in a hearse, and wrapped in the American flag. It was escorted by a small guard of cavalry, General Augur and other military officers following on foot.

A dense crowd accompanied the remains to the White House, where a military guard excluded the crowd, allowing none but persons of the household and personal friends of the deceased, to enter the premises, Senator Yates and Representative Farnsworth being among the number admitted.

The body is being embalmed with a view to its removal to Illinois. Flags over the Departments and throughout the city are all half mast. Scarcely any business is being transacted anywhere, either on private or public account.

Our citizens, without any preconcert whatever, are draping their premises with festoons of mourning.

The bells are tolling mournfully. All is the deepest gloom and sadness. Strong men weep in the streets. The grief is wide-spread and deep, and in strange contrast to the joy so lately manifested over our recent military victories.

This is indeed a day of gloom.

Reports prevail that Mr Frederick W. Seward who was kindly assisting in the nursing of Secretary Seward, received a stab in the back.

His shoulder blade prevented the knife or dagger from penetrating the body. The prospects are that he will recover.

A report is circulated, repeated by almost everybody, that Booth was captured fifteen miles this side of Baltimore. If it be true, as asserted, the War Department has received such information, it will, doubtless, be officially promulgated.

The Government departments are closed by order, and will be draped with the usual emblems of mourning.

The roads leading to and from the city are guarded by the military, and the utmost circumspection is observed as to all attempting to enter or leave the city.

The assassination of Republican Lincoln in April, 1865, placed Andrew Johnson in the White House. Both Democrats and Republicans were horrified by the death of Mr. Lincoln.

	Democrats	Republicans
President:	Horatio Seymour	Ulysses S. Grant
Vice-President:	Francis P. Blair, Jr.	Schuyler Colfax

HORATIO SEYMOUR,
THE DEMOCRATIC CANDIDATE FOR THE
PRESIDENCY.

Published by Frdr. Gerhard, 15 Dey St. New York City.

Horatio Seymour, popular Democratic governor of New York, presided as chairman of the Democratic convention that met in New York in 1868. It was Seymour whom the party ultimately nominated to run for president after a bitter three days of balloting. Actually, Seymour was pressed into the nomination against his will.

GRANT. COLFAX & VICTORY.
Pennsylvania 15,000! Ohio 25,000!!
The whole Democratic Party will make an Ascension in the Balloon, called
SEYMORE & BLAIR
DEPUTY SHERIFF, Capt.

SEE-MORE, BL(OW)AIR, after swinging around the circle, begging votes, taking their last BALOON ASCENSION with their Rebel Friends, and Sev-more's MOB constituents in New York City to the Salt Peter Caves.

This anti-Democratic broadside accused Seymour and his running mate, Francis P. Blair, Jr., of southern sympathies, because one leg of the Democratic platform was the restoration of states' rights in the Union with amnesty for political offenses during the Civil War. The mention of "Rebel Friends" in the small print of the broadside was an inflammatory phrase in many parts of the country.

SEYMOUR AND BLAIR'S

UNION

CAMPAIGN MARCH.
Chicago.
Published by Lyon & Healy, Clark & Washington Sts.

| Boston | New York | Philadelphia | St Paul |
| O. Ditson & Co. | C.H. Ditson & Co. | C.W.A. Trumpler | Munger Bros |

The Democratic "Campaign March" shown here pictures a handsome Seymour and a military Francis P. Blair, Jr. The choice of Blair for vice-president was one of the factors that caused the Democrats to lose the election to the popular Republican, Ulysses S. Grant. Blair had served as a general during the war, lived in the West, and previously had been a Republican. These were positive factors. However, they were overshadowed by the failure of his political speeches, which were frequently misconstrued to mean that he favored the overthrow of the new southern state governments.

CANDIDATE
FOR THE
Presidency

HORATIO SEYMOUR

CANDIDATE
FOR THE
Vice Presidency

GEN. FRANK P. BLAIR
1868

THE
Impendin Crisis uv the Dimocracy,

BEIN

A BREEF AND CONCISE STATEMENT UV THE
PAST EXPERIENCE, PRESENT CONDISH-
UN AND FUCHER HOPES UV THE
DIMOKRATIC PARTY:

INCLOODIN

THE MOST PROMINENT REESONS WHY EVRY DIMO-
KRAT WHO LOVES HIS PARTY SHOOD VOTE FOR

SEEMORE and BLARE, and agin GRANT and COLFAX.

By PETROLEUM V. NASBY,

Formerly Paster in charge of the Church of the Noo Dispensashun, late Perfesser uv
Biblikle Politics in the Southern Military and Classkle Institoot, and now
Postmaster at Confedrit X Roads, wich is in the State uv Kentucky

AMERICAN NEWS CO.,
119 & 121 NASSAU STREET,
NEW YORK.

The words on this pamphlet cover say vote for the Democrats. However, the spelling and general layout of the cover declare this to be a political spoof aimed at getting votes for the Republicans. The "fucher hopes uv the Dimokratic Party" went down the drain when the votes were counted in November.

Although Democrats wore presidential campaign ribbons like the one shown here, the party was too busy repudiating unfavorable publicity to win the election. The Reconstruction Acts in the platform were highly controversial, and even Seymour's popularity took a back seat to General Grant's promises of peace.

Snuff was a popular item at this time, so it was only natural that a political snuff box was sold to the faithful party members. Although these candidates were nominated in 1868, the dates on the box read 1869-1873, the dates Seymour and Blair would have served had they won the election.

"ONE VOTE LESS."—*Richmond Whig.*

The problem of the black vote was featured in this cartoon of a dead black man. Note the phrases on the wall that say "Seymour Ratification" and "KKK," showing this to be an anti-Democratic cartoon.

The banner carried here by those demonstrating for Seymour and Blair in New York says, "Reduce taxation before taxation reduces us." The military caps of many of the marchers indicate support from veterans of the Civil War. Since New York was Seymour's home state, it may be assumed that this torchlight parade was full of emotion for the state's own governor. Seymour did carry New York in the final vote for the presidency, but that victory was not enough to gain him entrance to the White House.

	Democrats	Republicans
President:	Horace Greeley	Ulysses S. Grant
Vice-President:	B. Gratz Brown	Henry Wilson

Ralph E. Becker Collection

The leading editor of the *New York Tribune,* Horace Greeley, supported many causes prior to his running for president in 1872. Temperance, women's rights, abolition of slavery, organization of labor, and having a protective tariff were all causes that he was involved in. If anything, Greeley was too intellectual. It was a simple matter for cartoonist Thomas Nast to ridicule Greeley, and he did so unmercifully.

The Democrats supported their candidate with sheet music bearing a distinguished picture of him. However, the opposition ridiculed Greeley's appearance, his metal rimmed spectacles, and his bald head. Greeley died, a crushed and broken man, shortly after losing the election in November.

Although this card was supposedly signed by Horace Greeley, it was anti-Greeley politics. The boat was headed for the "Salt River" or into the river with no ending. Aboard the vessel were "Liberals, Democrats, and Nancy's Friends," Nancy being the Democratic donkey, a future symbol of the Democratic Party.

GO WEST! GO WEST!! GO WEST!!!

The Boat having left Hynicka's Wharf on THURSDAY AFTERNOON, OCT 10, for "Salt River," and many stragglers having been left, a Regiment has been formed to leave here, by the UNDERGROUND RAILROAD, on

SATURDAY MORNING, AT 8 O'CLOCK.

LIBERALS, DEMOCRATS, and NANCY'S FRIENDS, pay Attention!

The following faithfuls have been selected as officers:

Colonel,	JOE KNIPE	Lieut. Colonel, - - JNO. H. FILLER
Major,	FOXY OSLER	Adjutant, - - J. C. M'ALARNEY
Surgeon,	DOC NEFF	Assistant Surgeon, - DOC RAHTER
Pay-Master,	FRANK ETTER	Chaplain, - - BILLY KNOCHE
Sergeant-Major,	SAM HUMMEL	Quarter-Master Seargeant, - DARBY BOYD
Hospital Steward,	BILL RODEARMEL	Cook, - - JIM SHRINER
Nurse, No. 1,	HARRY KRICHBAUM	Nurse, No. 2, JOE KAHNWEILER

High Privates, E. T. POSTLETHWAIT. BILL NICKOLS, FRANK SEILER, CHRIST FUNK, TOM NATHANS. MAJ. M'CONKEY, FRANK DEITRICK, FRED. HAEHNLEN, JAKEY RUPP, BILLY LESCURE, WALLY MAGLAUGHLIN, and others.

Regiment will form in front of Mayor's Office. Cameron's Menagerie will escort them to the Train. The Train will leave Dan Hocker's at 8 o'clock, sharp. Any one left behind will be court martialed.

Provisions on board of Train—SNITS, PRETZELS and WATER. By order.

HORACE GREELEY, Commander-in-Chief.

The Democratic convention was held in Baltimore in July. The scene shown here is outside of convention headquarters at Ford's Theatre. It was here that both Greeley and Brown of Missouri won the presidential and vice-presidential nominations.

This campaign card was put out by the Republican Party to show that "Nancy" the mule was not wanted in the House of Representatives. The unknown Cameron may or may not have made it into office, but this shows the type of opposition he faced.

I will Support all Republican Measures, but I will never Vote for Cameron! "Aleck said so." We guess not, Nancy.

"NANCY."

House of Representatives.

NO MULES ADMITTED HERE.

Greeley campaigned heavily in his losing battle against Grant. He is shown here addressing a large and enthusiastic gathering in the rain in Pittsburgh during a western tour.

Uncle Sam is shown here introducing Horace Greeley, "the champion of amnesty, peace and plenty to the sisterhood of states." The cartoon appeared in *Frank Leslie's Illustrated Newspaper* and was pro-Greeley. The artist dispensed with the caricatures of Greeley that appeared in opposition cartoons.

The problem of the Negro did not end with the Civil War. Even in 1872, Currier and Ives showed some of the "colored" legislators who served in Congress at that time. Most of the men pictured here were Southern Democrats.

Corruption existed at this time in the Democratic Party of New York and was to have an effect on national politics in the coming years. Boss Tweed is shown here looking at a blinded lady of justice.

This reconstruction cartoon of October, 1874,
was intended to show how the white man
intimidated the black voters. Although slavery was
no longer in existence, problems continued for
black people.

	Democrats	Republicans
President:	Samuel J. Tilden	Rutherford B. Hayes
Vice-President:	Thomas A. Hendricks	William A. Wheeler

This flag banner may well have been raised at the Democratic Convention in St. Louis in June, 1876. It shows the party's chosen candidates, Governor Samuel J. Tilden of New York for president and Governor Thomas A. Hendricks of Indiana for vice-president.

Parades were an ever popular method of rousing the voters to a high pitch of enthusiasm for the candidates. This paper lantern bearing Tilden's and Hendrick's names was typical of those used at the time.

The campaign sheet music did not convey to voters the Democratic Party platform, which was strongly aimed at reform in such areas as corruption, currency, tariff, and taxation. However, the "Grand March" was played wherever Democrats assembled as a means of getting out the vote.

These campaign badges are worthy of note, because both show the party symbol as the cock. The future symbol, the donkey, had not come into common use yet. The badge on the right was printed before the electoral commission had made their final vote and reflected what the Democrats believed would be the results of that vote, victory for Tilden and Hendricks.

Although early ballot returns on November 7 showed Tilden the winner, which even Hayes admitted in his personal diary, an electoral commission had to be appointed to settle this disputed election. On March 2, the final vote for president was counted giving Hayes 185 electoral votes and Tilden 184. The Democrats lost the presidency by just one electoral vote.

Since this election was so disputed, voting polls were still being shown in *Frank Leslie's Illustrated Newspaper* on December 2, 1876. Elephant Johnie's was a famous voting poll in New Orleans. Note the deputy marshal's badge on the black man with a billy stick.

This self-portrait of Thomas Nast, drawn in 1879, shows a caricature of the man who originated the Democratic donkey symbol in one of his cartoons. Nast was a political cartoonist who achieved notoriety through his biting sarcasm. He wielded a mighty pen, which affected both major parties in politics.

	Democrats	Republicans
President:	Winfield S. Hancock	James A. Garfield
Vice-President:	William H. English	Chester A. Arthur

The Democratic convention of 1880 took place in Cincinnati, Ohio, and the platform adopted by the party stressed home rule and honest money, as well as the subordination of the military to the civil power.

HANCOCK AND ENGLISH,
...1880...

General Winfield S. Hancock, presidential nominee, was a fifty-six year old professional soldier from Pennsylvania. William H. English, his running mate, was a well-to-do banker and former congressman from Indiana. Hancock's military record was considered a plus because it matched that of Garfield, the Republican candidate for president.

A wooden mechanical rooster, symbol of the Democratic Party, was seen feeding the ballot box with votes for the Democratic candidate. This rooster was used in parades in support of Han-cock.

This political novelty of 1880 was a play on the presidential candidate's name — the hand being for Han and the party symbol of the cock completing the name Hancock. The Republican newspaper said to be presenting the novelty must have been supporting the Democrats in this election.

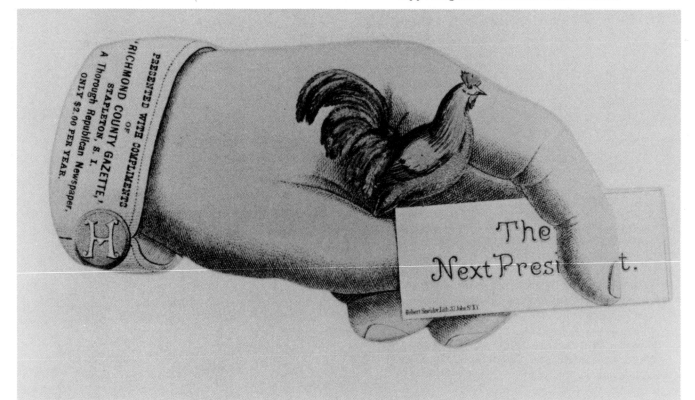

PRESENTED WITH COMPLIMENTS
OF
"RICHMOND COUNTY GAZETTE,"
STAPLETON, S. I.
A Thorough Republican Newspaper,
ONLY $2.00 PER YEAR.

H

The Next President.

In nominating Hancock and English, shown here on a typical Democratic bandanna of the day, the Democrats took into account sectional prejudices. Hancock was from Pennsylvania, while English made his home in Indiana, so the party hoped to attract voters from all parts of the country.

This flag banner for Hancock and English bears thirty-nine stars. The country was still growing and the bright, colorful flag was still one of the strongest vote-getting symbols around.

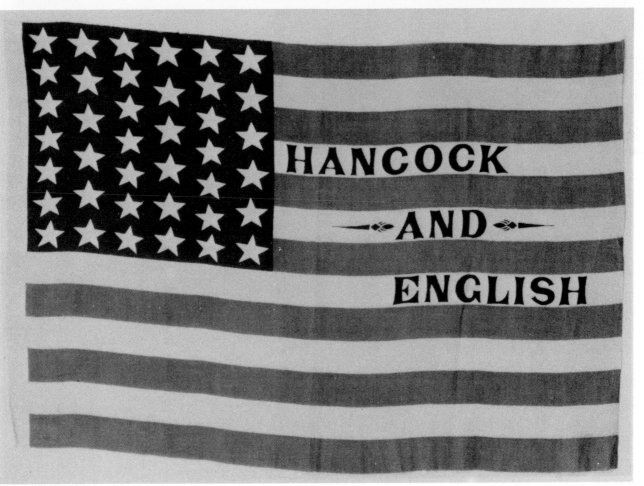

HANCOCK
◆—AND—◆
ENGLISH

Most pictures show General Hancock in the formal attire he wears here. Although this sheet music describes a "rousing campaign song," this was not as fiery an election as some others. It ended in defeat for the Democratic Party.

Campaign textiles, like the one shown here, were usually red, white, and blue like the American flag. Once again, Hancock is shown in a rather formal attire, as is his running mate, William H. English.

Although James A. Garfield won the election of 1880 for the Republicans, he did not serve out his term in office. An assassin's bullet wounded the President on July 3, 1881. Death followed seventy-nine days later on September 10, 1881. Chester A. Arthur, the vice-president, then assumed the presidency to finish out the term. The loss of support within his own party cost Arthur the nomination for president in 1884.

	Democrats	Republicans
President:	Grover Cleveland	James G. Blaine
Vice-President:	Thomas A. Hendricks	John A. Logan

Grover Cleveland was nominated as the Democratic candidate at the party convention in Chicago on July 8. He won the nomination with the support of his home state, New York. Even the famous R. H. Macy & Co. put its name and advertisement on "Cleveland's Grand March." Note the ad for muslin underwear in the small print.

Cleveland and his running mate, Thomas A. Hendricks, are shown on this party broadside, as is the adopted platform of the party. The Democrats hoped for "prosperity to our common country, Reform, Purity and Honesty." Biographies of both candidates are in very small print beside their pictures.

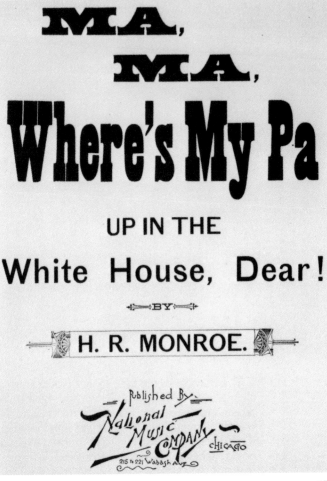

This sheet music is an example of the mudslinging that went on during the campaign of 1884. The question on it refers to a widow who named Cleveland as the father of her illegitimate child in 1874. Cleveland accepted the responsibility, perhaps to shield others involved, and made some financial arrangements for the child. Eventually, due to the mother's misconduct, the child was placed in an orphanage, from which he was later adopted; he then faded from the public scene.

The innocent-looking child pictured here was supposed to have been fathered by Grover Cleveland. Although these charges were widely publicized during the campaign, it was never proved that Cleveland was the father. Few people even knew of the matter until it appeared in print in 1884.

HOW BLAINE GREW RICH IN OFFICE.

BLAINE'S HOUSE IN AUGUSTA, 1862.

BLAINE'S MANSION IN WASHINGTON.
(See the Other Side.)

The Democrats did their share of mudslinging with this anti-Blaine campaign poster. Blaine was reputed to have made his money during a railroad scandal some years before he was nominated by the Republican Party. He was supposed to have gotten rich enough to move to his own Washington mansion.

PROGRAM
AFTER 24 YEARS.

For the especial amusement of the Black Reps. the following program has been arranged on vessel No. I, viz.:

Under the following Management.

Compass, ...J. M. W. G.
Log Book, ...J. B. W.
Whisky Bottle, ...J. A. H.
Slop Tub, ...Josh L.
Sole Proprietor, ...C. Revenue E.
Bill Poster, ...Billy D, Esq.

ACT I.
THE GRAND KICK.
A PATHETIC MELO-DRAMA, IN ONE ACT.

Kicker, ...Grover C.
Kicked, ...24-year Suckers out of Office.

ACT II.
THE ROGUE'S MARCH.

Illustrating the Mournful Procession of "Two Dollars apiece at the Election Polls," following the remains of the "Tariff Scare" to its final Resting Place.

Orator, ...Reverend Matthew Molten Diggs
Pall Bearers—Samuel Allen, Nosey Halback, Jno. Copland, Honorable Henry Demuth, Senior, Esq., Mr. All Edwards, Mr. Jack-ass Bailey, etc.
Undertaker, ...Clayton Meyers.
Hearse Driver, ...Benjamin Franklin Eshleman.
Drivers—Bobby Robinson, Petey Fordney, Bucky Leibley, F. R. Diffenderfer, Jackey Heistand accompanied by Brave "Joshey the Groomsman," A. H. Peacock, J. W. Johnson, W. B. Middleton, Nosey Shay, Christ Stoner, E. K. Martin, Jimmy Landis, Jimmy G. Blaine and John A. Logan.

For the Loan of a Set of Furniture, the Famous Walter Kieffer will write the Obituary Notices.

The program shown on this card had much meaning for the readers of 1884. Today, the play in which Grover C. was featured as the Kicker has faded into obscurity and much of the meaning of the opposition to the Democrats has as well.

Trade or advertising cards, such as the ones shown here, were a means of promoting the candidate and the product at the same time. These cards were given away with cigarettes by W. Duke Sons & Co. of Durham, North Carolina, and New York. One of the cards reads proudly — "Our average sales are over two million per day."

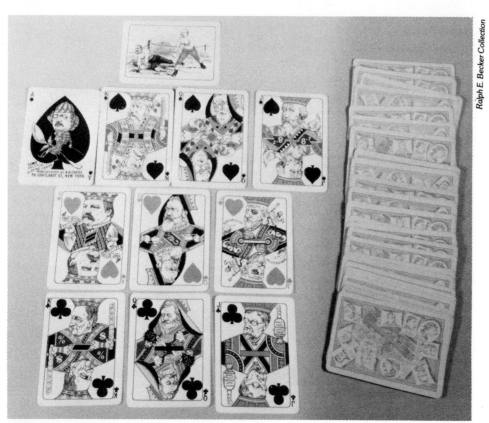

Each of these political playing-card faces represented someone prominent in politics during this election year. The King of Spades represented Grover Cleveland, while the Queen of Hearts was James Blaine. The front side of these "comic political playing cards" showed various prominent newspapers of the day with pictures of their editors.

Cleveland is pictured here carrying a sword for free trade. The *Judge* magazine cartoon caption reads, "Grover, the giant-killer, undertakes a big contract," implying that he was too small to fight big business. Note Cleveland's small moustache in a day when most men wore full beards.

We may differ in Politics   but We all agree that.

This cartoon shows the two major parties in a united front on the issue of prohibition in 1884. Democratic candidate Grover Cleveland and Republican candidate James Blaine are seated here together at a table where hard liquor is being served.

Republican Blaine's morals were as much, if not more, in question as Cleveland's. This political discussion in a country store was "the main point of controversy between conservative and progressive Republicans." A rainstorm in upstate New York may have swung the final votes to the Democrats, as the rain prevented many rural Republicans from getting to the polls. The cities were all predominantly Democratic and for Cleveland.

	Democrats	Republicans
President:	Grover Cleveland	Benjamin Harrison
Vice-President:	Allen G. Thurman	Levi P. Morton

The bachelor President Cleveland married the young and beautiful Frances Folsom while he was president. His wife was a definite asset when he ran for office again, but not quite strong enough to put Cleveland back in the White House. Advertising cards, such as this one by the Merrick Thread Company, were widely distributed during the course of the unsuccessful campaign.

"When Grover Goes Marching Home" was music sung by enough Republicans to keep Cleveland from a second term in office. The opposition was toward his foreign and domestic policies and his lack of action on the tariff question. The Republicans were strongly in favor of a protective tariff to "support the interests of America."

When Grover Goes Marching Home.

REPUBLICAN CAMPAIGN SONGS
1888.
MALE QUARTETT.
Arranged by R. CAMPAIGN.

40

PUBLISHED BY
S. BRAINARD'S SONS,
CLEVELAND AND CHICAGO.

A THANKSGIVING DINNER À LA DAMOCLES.

Cleveland's growing popularity was supposed to be the sword hanging over the heads of Republican candidates Harrison and Morton. Since there was little division at the Democratic National Convention held in St. Louis on June 5, Cleveland easily won the nomination, which the magazine *PUCK* felt proved his popularity.

These tickets up the Salt River were intended to be a journey to oblivion for the Democrats. The steamer was called ''Free Trade,'' since the free trade issue was one of the most important in this election. Domestic industry was concerned that the lack of a protective tariff would allow foreign companies to undersell American goods.

The beehives shown in this *Judge* cartoon were making things hot for Cleveland and vice-presidential candidate Thurman. "The noble old Roman," as seventy-five year old Thurman was frequently called, is shown here waving his red bandanna. It was said that he always used a red handkerchief "both for blowing his nose and dipping snuff."

This Harrison and Morton paper lantern showed the Republican candidates' use of an earlier slogan from 1840 — now it went "Tippecanoe and Morton too."

The *Judge* cartoonist portrays Cleveland replacing his first vice-president by putting Allen Thurman of Ohio in harness. Thurman was a very popular if elderly figure, well known for his red pocket handkerchief, which became his symbol. He replaced Cleveland's first vice-president, Thomas Hendricks, who died, according to this cartoon, of the hard work he did for Cleveland's election in 1884.

Thurman's red bandanna is used again in this cartoon to sail the ship of state. Cleveland, who was a very big man, is portrayed as too heavy to keep the ship afloat.

Although the party platform promised a free trade policy, the voters did not vote for Cleveland. The aged Thurman is shown here being carried by Cleveland and, once again, a red bandanna hangs from his pocket.

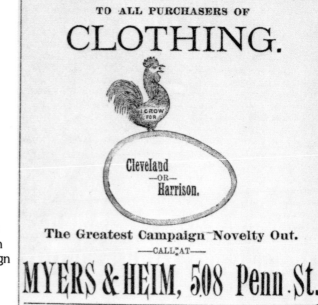

This campaign novelty was offered in the *Daily Times and Dispatch* of Reading, Pennsylvania, on November 8, 1888. Billed as the greatest campaign novelty, an egg with the candidate of the voter's choice on it was presented free to anyone who purchased clothing at the store.

Free whiskey was offered by those who electioneered for both parties in the Rocky Mountains in an effort to gain votes. Campaign rallies such as the one shown here were aimed at getting out the rural vote.

Captain Nicholas Costello was probably the oldest citizen to cast his vote for Grover Cleveland. The gentleman with the top hat and the high-laced shoes claimed to be 106 years old and voted for Cleveland and Thurman on November 6, 1888. Even the support of this centenarian was not enough to put Cleveland back into the White House.

	Democrats	Republicans
President:	Grover Cleveland	Benjamin Harrison
Vice-President:	Adlai E. Stevenson	Whitelaw Reid

The Democratic convention of 1892 was held in the Wigwam Building in Chicago on June 21. This picture, bordered with pictures of prominent delegates to that convention, shows both the interior and exterior of the building.

An artist's sketch shows the excitement among those attending the national convention when Grover Cleveland's name was put into nomination. The former president, who had at first seemed unwilling to run, was a logical and popular choice to carry the party standard back into the White House.

The Democratic candidates, pictured on this cotton bandanna, were Grover Cleveland of New York and Adlai E. Stevenson, a former first assistant postmaster general and an experienced politician. The words "Tariff Reform" printed on this banner reflected one of the major issues of the campaign.

Frances Cleveland, pictured here on a woven Jacquard ribbon, was a popular figure and a political asset to her husband. She was one of the first women to have any political clout at all, since this was a time when women were expected to remain in the home.

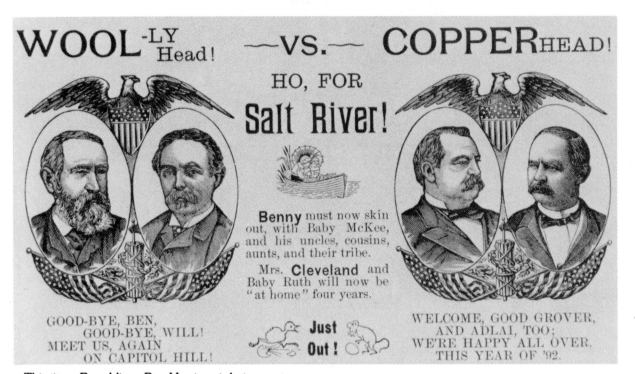

WOOL-LY Head! — VS. — COPPER HEAD!

HO, FOR Salt River!

Benny must now skin out, with Baby McKee, and his uncles, cousins, aunts, and their tribe.

Mrs. **Cleveland** and Baby Ruth will now be "at home" four years.

GOOD-BYE, BEN,
GOOD-BYE, WILL!
MEET US, AGAIN
ON CAPITOL HILL!

Just Out!

WELCOME, GOOD GROVER,
AND ADLAI, TOO;
WE'RE HAPPY ALL OVER,
THIS YEAR OF '92.

This time, Republican Ben Harrison is being sent up the Salt River to political oblivion. Grover Cleveland, who had left politics after his presidential defeat in 1888, gave up his lucrative law practice in New York to return to the national political scene.

The "seated" figure here is Benjamin Harrison, and the question posed by the cartoonist refers to the Republican nomination for president. The other men waiting behind Harrison were probably possible candidates. Grover Cleveland, with the Capitol symbolically behind him, was looking in the window at the scene.

WHO IS NEXT?

Tariff reform was one of the most explosive issues in this campaign. Cleveland favored revising existing tariff laws without harming existing domestic industries. Other issues shown in this cartoon include free silver coinage, farmer alliance, and prohibition — the latter being shown by a woman carrying an umbrella.

Frances Cleveland was married to the bachelor president on June 2, 1886, during Cleveland's first term of office. By 1892 the popular Frances is shown on this deck of playing cards as the Queen of Diamonds. Grover Cleveland is the King, and the Jack represents Benjamin Harrison. The Joker crows of victory for the Democrats.

The man standing on the stump in this Nebraska logging camp is William Jennings Bryan, a man who would appear as a popular political figure in future presidential campaigns. The ardent Democrat was undoubtedly speaking here on behalf of Grover Cleveland.

This parade for Grover Cleveland, after his election and return to the White House, was a gala celebration. Note the campaign banner across the street with pictures of both Democratic candidates on it. Behind the campaign banner hangs an American flag, but despite the banners across the street, all eyes are turned toward the candidate in his high top hat.

	Democrats	Republicans
President:	William Jennings Bryan	William McKinley
Vice-President:	Arthur Sewall	Garret A. Hobart

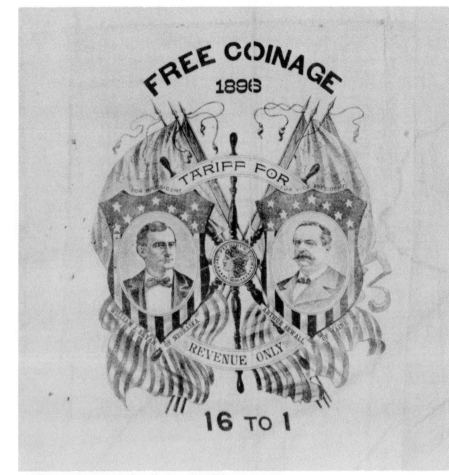

"Free coinage of silver" plus "tariff for revenue only" were the planks that carried William Jennings Bryan into the Democratic nomination for president in 1896. Arthur Sewall of Maine was named as vice-presidential candidate, and he too was a free silver advocate.

William McKinley, the Republican governor of Ohio who was backed by politician Mark Hanna, favored the gold standard. The economic panic and depression that took place during Cleveland's term of office hindered the Democrats in this election and helped the Republicans to victory.

THIS DISC, which is same thickness as Standard Silver Dollar, represents in size, 796 Grains Coin Silver, which is the Equivalent of ONE GOLD DOLLAR. August, 1896.

THE VERDICT OF THE IMMORTAL DEAD
What can Hanna and the Gold Standard Advocate say in reply to LINCOLN GARFIELD and BLAINE?

Mark Hanna is shown here as the power behind the Republican candidate, seated by Hanna's left arm. This anti-Republican cartoon was aimed at the defeat of the gold-standard advocates.

GENERAL GRANT'S SON FOR BRYAN

"If my father could vote today he would vote for Bryan for President of the United States."

The above words are from the lips of Jesse Grant, favorite son of Gen. U.S. Grant. The son has left the Republican Party just as his father before him left the Democratic Party when it made a compromise with the slave power. In his farewell to the Republican Party Jesse Grant writes:

"I believe honestly in the great advantage to this country of the free coinage of silver. It does not mean repudiation of our debts at home or abroad. These debts will have to be paid in products, and anything that will raise the value of them will, I believe, benefit all classes. If we can double the price of a silver rupee we have doubled the price of the wheat that comes in competition with our wheat, and therefore double our wheat as to its debt paying capacity. The same argument holds good of the silver peso of the Latin-American countries, and the price of our meats and live stock. It holds good, too, in the silver ruble and the price of oil. It holds good in many ways too numerous to mention.

"Instead of foreigners purchasing the product of our silver mines at the rate of 70 cents per ounce, and with this silver buying produce, some of which comes in direct competition with our productions, from South America and the orient, they would have to pay at the rate of $1.29 per ounce.

"As to repudiation, why, we have practically repudiated already, if bankruptcy means failure to pay debts. Did you ever think of what an awful debt America owes today? Nineteen thousand millions of mortgaged indebtedness. All the gold and silver in the world would not pay one-third of this single item of mortgage indebtedness, and under our present arrangement of things the awful disparagement between the ability to produce and the power of money to accumulate interest makes the breach between this country and solvency grow wider every year. Prices go down, money going up. Interest eating, eating all the time. How can it ever be paid? The free coinage of silver I do not believe to be a panacea for all our evils, but I do believe it a step in the right direction and for the best interest of the American people."

Signed, JESSE GRANT.

P. S—Of course, Mark Hanna and his multimillionaire campaign committee are calling Jesse Grant an anarchist, a repudiator, a thief and a scoundrel. Let the people vote Hanna and his crowd out of existence November 3d. If they don't, they will never get another chance.

To gain Republican votes, this Bryan poster shows the son of a famous Republican president supporting the Democratic William Jennings Bryan. The son asserts that his father would have voted for the "silver-tongued orator." Jesse Grant declared, "The free coinage of silver I do not believe to be a panacea for all our evils, but I do believe it a step in the right direction and for the best interest of the American people."

PULL FOR YOUR CANDIDATE

The campaign novelty shown here features the Democratic donkey. When the donkey's tail was pulled, the picture of candidate Bryan appeared.

STICK A PIN HERE.

Bryan
AND
Free Silver
16 TO 1

Mark, Hanna, what we say:
The Flag of our Country
waves for ALL our people.

Election Day, November 3, '96

Free silver was featured on campaign ribbons as was the idea that the silver standard would benefit all factions of the nation. The six new states admitted to the Union between 1889 and 1890 strengthened the cause of the silver advocates.

DUBIOUS.

"What awful poor wages they get in all those free silver countries, John!"
"That's so, wife, but the politicians say it will be different in America."
"I wouldn't take any chances on it, John. It's easy to lower wages and hard to raise them. Politicians will tell you anything. We know there was good wages when we had protection. We could never buy clothes for the children on what they get in those free silver countries, could we?"

The feeling against free silver ran as high as the feeling for it. The reprint from *Wasp* features the Republican reasons for staying on the gold standard.

The political drinking mug shown here was a bartender's delight. A picture of Bryan on one side and a picture of McKinley on the other made this novelty acceptable to either party. If the drinker was a Democrat, Bryan's picture was turned toward him. If the drinker was Republican, he was served with McKinley facing him.

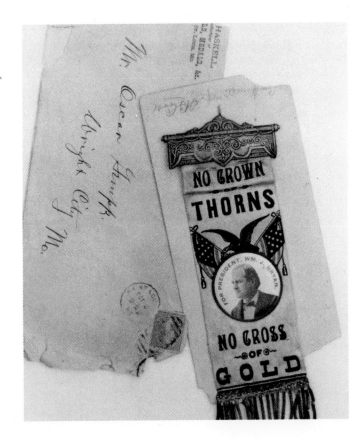

Democrats wore party badges like the one shown here that says, "No crown of thorns . . . no cross of gold" and has Bryan's picture under the eagle and the flag. The main party issue for this campaign was free coinage of silver.

William Jennings Bryan was nominated by the Democratic Party in Chicago on July 7, 1896. Two views of the exterior of the convention hall are shown here.

This is how William Jennings Bryan looked when he received the Democratic nomination. His talents as a public speaker drew audiences to him as long as he remained on the public scene.

This campaign whistle-stop at Crest Line, Ohio, shows the presidential hopeful Bryan with his wife. The train, en route to New York, made many stops to allow the people to meet Mr. Bryan. Despite his personal popularity, Bryan lost the election of 1896.

President:	Democrats	Republicans
President:	William Jennings Bryan	William McKinley
Vice-President:	Adlai E. Stevenson	Theodore Roosevelt

In 1900 the Democratic National Convention was held in Kansas City on July 4th. The patriotic campaign bandanna here shows the winning candidates to be Bryan for president and Stevenson, who ran once before for the same office, as vice president.

Free silver was still a disputed plank within the Democratic Party but Bryan continued his free silver campaign. He ordered this paperweight to be made from scrap metal, and it was his personal possession. Although Bryan had supported the Spanish-American War and served as a colonel, he favored the peace treaty and denounced imperialism abroad.

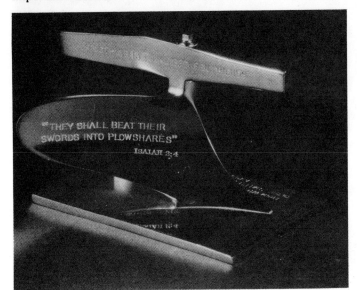

This Democratic campaign tumbler, today a collector's item, was a common novelty in 1900. The picture of Bryan seems more like the young Bryan of 1896.

TAKE YOUR CHOICE OF THE TWO BILLS!

Judge magazine supported the Republicans in this campaign by showing the full dinner pail symbolizing prosperity coming from McKinley's gold standard. Bryan's dollar, on the silver standard, would only be worth fifty-three cents. The cartoon was headed with the words, "We want no change."

This Republican campaign poster showed what the Republicans had to say about the past four years of Republican policies. It was their claim that the American flag had been placed on foreign soil for humanity's sake, not for the acquisition of more territory. The Democrats of the day condemned Republican foreign policy, labeling it as imperialism.

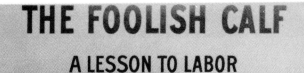

THE FOOLISH CALF
A LESSON TO LABOR

WHILE BEING DRIVEN HOME ONE EVENING BY A BOY, A FOOLISH CALF LEFT ITS MOTHER AND RAN AFTER A BELLOWING STEER. THE BOY TRIED IN VAIN TO BRING IT BACK TO ITS MOTHER'S SIDE, WHEN, FINALLY EXHAUSTED, HE SHOOK HIS FIST AT THE CALF AND CRIED: "YOU LITTLE FOOL, YOU LITTLE FOOL, YOU, YOU——FOOL, YOU'LL BE SORRY WHEN SUPPER TIME COMES."

MORAL—REMEMBER THE HARD TIMES OF 1896. DON'T BE A BRYAN CALF AND GET STEERED AWAY FROM THE FULL DINNER PAIL, OR "YOU'LL BE SORRY WHEN SUPPER TIME COMES."

The Democrats were badly hurt by the "full dinner pail" campaign of the Republican Party. This poster reminds the voters of the hard times of 1896 and the prosperity that came to the country under the McKinley regime.

This picture appeared in *Harper's* on July 14, 1900, and shows the delegates at the Democratic convention held earlier in July. The bust of Bryan on the speaker's platform undoubtedly brought forth many cheers from the assembled people.

Theodore Roosevelt, shown here campaigning in his top hat and horse-drawn carriage, was a familiar sight all over the country during his political career. Theodore Roosevelt assumed the presidency after the death of President McKinley on September 14, 1901.

	Democrats	Republicans
President:	Alton B. Parker	Theodore Roosevelt
Vice-President:	Henry G. Davis	Charles W. Fairbanks

FOR PRESIDENT
ALTON B. PARKER
OF NEW YORK

FOR VICE-PRESIDENT
HENRY G. DAVIS
OF WEST VIRGINIA

Alton B. Parker, chief justice of the New York Court of Appeals, was nominated as the Democratic candidate for president in an effort to gain the important New York votes. His running mate was to be Henry G. Davis of West Virginia.

Note the difference in age between Parker and Senator Davis. The senator, who was nominated on the first vice-presidential ballot at the July convention in St. Louis, was eighty years old at the time and called by some "a ruin from West Virginia." Davis ended up living to be ninety-two years old.

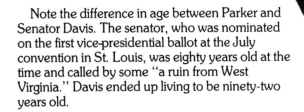

DEMOCRATIC CANDIDATES 1904
PARKER and DAVIS

Although the Democratic Party platform sidestepped the issue of free silver at this time, Parker threw a bombshell when he announced that he favored the gold standard. This fact, plus the popularity of the "Rough Rider" Roosevelt, was one of the factors that cost Parker the election.

This lithograph of Booker T. Washington and Theodore Roosevelt dining together at the White House was used as campaign propaganda by both parties. The North portrayed Mr. Washington looking more Caucasian than black and therefore acceptable as a guest in the White House. The African looks portrayed by the South made him seem unacceptable. This was a particularly ugly type of political mudslinging used to promote views for and against the racial issue. The picture also appeared on campaign buttons of the day.

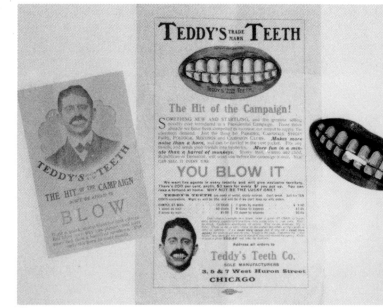

This campaign novelty was intended to be blown for the Republican candidate, yet the advertisement reads, "Every man, woman or child, Republican or Democrat, will want one before the campaign is over."

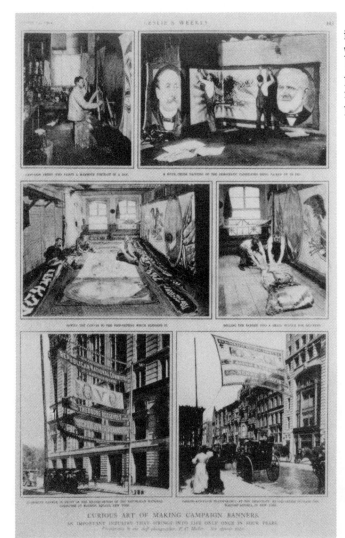

Along with national party conventions, an industry that "springs into life only once in four years" is the making of campaign banners. *Leslie's Weekly* featured this industry in a start-to-finish picture series in its October 13, 1904, issue. Both major party banners are shown in the final two pictures.

The issue of prohibition was destined to be an emotional and controversial issue until it was repealed in February 1933. This cartoon, circa 1904, contrasts the evil appearance of the brewer with the innocence of the mother and children. Prohibitionists, who formed a minor political party, frequently tried to place pressure on major party candidates.

1908

Democrats
President: William Jennings Bryan
Vice-President: John W. Kern

Republicans
William H. Taft
James S. Sherman

The Democratic candidates for 1908 were the still popular William Jennings Bryan for president and John Worth Kern for vice-president. Although they ran against several minor party candidates — such as those from the Socialist Labor Party and the Prohibitionists — the Republican candidates, William Howard Taft and his running mate James S. Sherman, were their major opposition.

FOR PRESIDENT
WILLIAM JENNINGS BRYAN

FOR VICE-PRESIDENT
JOHN W. KERN

Ralph E. Becker Collection

UNCLE SAM—"MR BRYAN, YOUR ENEMIES ARE MINE ALSO."

One of Bryan's major issues in this campaign was his opposition to the trust magnates. He contended that big business was harmful to the economy and was only interested in its own profits. This cartoon was aimed directly at the trust magnates, and showed that Bryan and Uncle Sam were both interested in the little man.

The china plate shown here with its bold picture of William Jennings Bryan was a typical campaign souvenir in 1908.

Campaign novelties such as these pictures of Bryan were intended to arouse strong emotions. Comparing Bryan to the country's first president was intended to gain votes for the Democratic candidate. Even if it succeeded in gaining some emotional votes, it did not win enough votes to insure victory for the Democrats in this election.

Grand in Peace, Brave in War,
Lovingly in the Hearts of His Countrymen.

First in Peace, First in War,
First in the Hearts of His Countrymen.

Copyright, 1908, by John M. Jones

W J Bryan

Copyright, 1908, by John M. Jones   Stuart 1754-182

G Washington

THE ENTHRONED HOG.

· TRUST · REX ·

"SHALL THE PEOPLE RULE?"
WILLIAM JENNINGS BRYAN.

The party in power, the Republicans under Theodore Roosevelt, were accused repeatedly of corruption by the Democrats. This particular cartoon may have been aimed at Republican Senator Foraker and Governor Haskell of Oklahoma, who were both known to have had intimate dealings with the Standard Oil Company, one of the nation's largest trust companies.

The Democratic Convention of 1908, which nominated William Jennings Bryan for president, began in the auditorium in Denver, Colorado, on July 7.

Where the Democratic Convention will be held

Photographs by Brown Brothers

Both major candidates campaigned in New York City in 1908, and this picture shows the newest means of talking directly to the people — the phonograph.

Campaigning methods in 1908 included the use of trains and automobiles as well as arranged platform speeches. Here are samples of the methods used by the candidates. William Howard Taft is shown on a campaign tour by train. The Socialist candidate, Eugene V. Debs, also used a train for campaigning. John W. Kern, James S. Sherman, and Bryan are all shown making speeches directly to the people.

THE CHIEF CONTESTANTS

THE REPUBLICAN CANDIDATE, William Howard Taft, went on an extensive campaign tour which carried him through the Middle Western and Western States. Here he delivers a speech from the back of his special train.

THE SOCIALIST CANDIDATE, Eugene V. Debs, campaigned extensively in his train, nicknamed "The Red Special." He visited many parts of the country, making speeches to propagate the Socialist party program.

TAFT CAMPAIGNING in an automobile. In the back seat of beflagged vehicle sits the venerable Gen. Keifer.

JOHN W. KERN, the Democratic vice-presidential candidate, accepts the nomination in a speech at Indianapolis.

JAMES S. SHERMAN, the Republican vice-presidential nominee, delivers his acceptance speech at Utica, N. Y.

WILLIAM J. BRYAN, the choice of the Democrats for the Presidency, accepts the nomination at Lincoln, Neb.

1912

	Democrats	Republicans	Progressive (Bull Moose)
President:	Woodrow Wilson	William H. Taft	Theodore Roosevelt
Vice-President:	Thomas R. Marshall	James S. Sherman	Hiram W. Johnson

Perhaps one of the most contested Democratic National Conventions of all time was the one that began in Baltimore on July 25, 1912. The main contest for president was between Champ Clark of Missouri and Woodrow Wilson of New Jersey. It took forty-seven ballots and a long convention fight before Woodrow Wilson was finally chosen.

ELKHART IND.

FOR PRESIDENT
WOODROW WILSON
OF
NEW JERSEY.

FOR VICE PRESIDENT
THOMAS R. MARSHALL
OF
INDIANA.

Two governors were to carry the Democratic banner for 1912 and win the election. Woodrow Wilson was governor of New Jersey while his running mate, Thomas R. Marshall, was governor of Indiana.

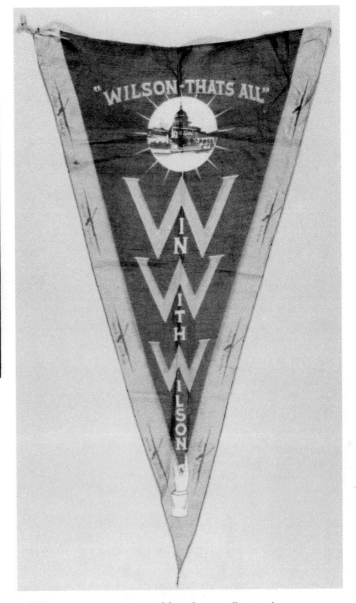

The picture of Woodrow Wilson on this 1912 kerchief shows a distinguished-looking candidate. Wilson had been president of Princeton University, and he proved himself to be far more than just a scholar by giving stirring campaign speeches. The speeches may not have had much meat in them but they inspired his listeners with confidence.

Wilson pennants were sold and seen all over the country as the candidate campaigned. Had there not been a division in the Republican Party, Wilson's campaign might not have been as successful as it was. However, the three W's did get Woodrow Wilson into the White House, the first Democrat to go to Washington as president since 1892.

These campaign ribbons show what was happening to the country politically in 1912. Wilson defeated Champ Clark at the Democratic National Convention. Theodore Roosevelt withdrew from the Republican Convention — which nominated Taft — and formed the Progressive Party, also called the Bull Moose Party (so called because T.R. once declared, "I'm feeling like a bull moose!"). This split among the once solid Republicans certainly helped Wilson win the election.

The three major candidates for the presidency are shown as they campaigned by train. From left to right, they are Woodrow Wilson, Theodore Roosevelt, and William Howard Taft.

Woodrow Wilson is being interviewed here while on a campaign trip. The interviewer is holding a camera in his hands while he questions the candidate.

I THINK WE'VE GOT ANOTHER WASHINGTON AND WILSON IS HIS NAME

This campaign poster would have been appropriate in either 1912 or 1916. Comparing Wilson to George Washington was an attempt to convince the voters that the professor-politician was as competent as the Father of Our Country.

	Democrats	Republicans
President:	Woodrow Wilson	Charles E. Hughes
Vice-President:	Thomas R. Marshall	Charles W. Fairbanks

Patriotic songs on behalf of Woodrow Wilson were sung loud and clear after he was nominated again by the Democrats at their national convention in St. Louis. The June convention stressed that Wilson had kept the country out of World War I. This sheet music likened Wilson to Washington and Lincoln.

This poster for "America's Leader" stressed the idea that Wilson was a fine statesman as well as a true patriot. The country hoped and believed that Woodrow Wilson was the man to keep the United States neutral during World War I.

Wilson made comparatively few campaign speeches, but when he did speak, this picture caption says, his lucid arguments won him both friends and votes.

WILSON MADE VERY FEW SPEECHES, BUT HIS LUCID ARGUMENTS WON HIM FRIENDS AND VOTES.

Election day was November 7 and as usual was on a Tuesday. It took until Thursday before the country and Wilson knew that the people of California had cast their votes for the Democratic candidate. This sheet music refers to those deciding votes. Written in small print in the chorus are the lines, "And don't forget 'twas votes for women helped to win the vict'ry, too."

Woman's suffrage was gaining importance as an issue for both parties at this time. The women shown here are standing outside the White House grounds attempting to make their voices and wishes better known to the President and the country as well.

	Democrats	Republicans
President:	James M. Cox	Warren G. Harding
Vice-President:	Franklin D. Roosevelt	Calvin Coolidge

When the Democratic Party met for its convention in June, President Wilson was an invalid in the White House. The party's chosen candidates were James M. Cox, governor of Ohio, and Franklin Delano Roosevelt, the young assistant secretary of the Navy. The platform endorsed Wilson's stand on the controversial League of Nations and blamed post-war problems on the Republicans.

Warren G. Harding, the Republican nominee for president, is shown in this wooden model wearing a top hat. This campaign novelty was called a "nose-thumber" for obvious reasons. The wooden arm moved up and down when the tail was pulled.

This "Cox for President" beanie was worn by many of the party faithful during the 1920 campaign. Peace, progress, and prosperity were featured on other campaign material of the day.

This picture of the vice-presidential candidate shows Franklin Delano Roosevelt before he was afflicted with polio. His good looks and pleasing manner were both assets, as was the well-known and still popular Roosevelt name. Although Theodore Roosevelt had not been a Democrat, the force of his personality probably gave some votes to his young cousin.

Warren G. Harding, the Republican who won the presidency in 1920, became ill and died in San Francisco on August 2, 1923. Calvin Coolidge assumed the office of president at this time.

THE OFFICIAL REPUBLICAN CAMPAIGN SONG

HARDING
You're The Man For Us

WARREN G. HARDING
Republican Candidate for President

CALVIN COOLIDGE
Republican Candidate for Vice President

Words and Music by

AL JOLSON

30

	Democrats	Republicans
President:	John W. Davis	Calvin Coolidge
Vice-President:	Charles W. Bryan	Charles G. Dawes

Ralph E. Becker Collection

The National Democratic Convention at Madison Square Garden had more fireworks than the campaign that followed it. Such names as William Gibbs McAdoo, son-in-law of Woodrow Wilson, and Al Smith, governor of New York, were thrown into nomination. The Ku Klux Klan reemerged at this time and became a political force at the convention. Emotions ran high and there was much flag-waving.

Governor Al Smith of New York was cheered loudly when his name was put up in nomination. Because he was Catholic and a product of Tammany, he was fought by the Klan. Prohibitionists fought him too, as he was definitely a "wet." With all of this strong opposition, Al Smith did not gain the nomination for president.

John W. Davis of West Virginia was an able Wall Street lawyer and an eastern conservative. He had been a member of Congress and served as solicitor general and as ambassador to Great Britain. When the smoke of the convention cleared, Davis had won the nomination over all other nominees. The brother of William Jennings Bryan, Governor Charles W. Bryan of Nebraska, was Davis' running mate.

The main thrust of the 1924 campaign was against the Republican scandals that took place during Harding's administration. That is why justice, equality, and honesty were stressed in this broadside, which appeared on the back of Democratic sheet music for Davis.

WHAT JOHN W. DAVIS BELIEVES

JUSTICE AND EQUALITY

"There must be not only an equality of opportunity and equality of right, but an equality of burden in this country; no law that favors one class above another; that takes the burden from the shoulders of one to put it upon his neighbors, is consonant with American ideals or American traditions."

HONESTY

"I indict the Republican Party in its organized capacity for having shaken public confidence to its very foundation. I ask the voters throughout the land to pass judgment of condemnation, as a warning to all men who may aspire to public office, that dishonestly either in thought, word or deed will not be tolerated in America."

John W. Davis

Paperweights, bearing the likeness of John W. Davis, were made for this presidential campaign.

By 1924 there were enough automobiles in use to warrant the making of this license plate attachment.

This Coolidge presidential campaign decal was circulated by the Republicans. Coolidge's reputation as an honest man from New England was strong enough to override the Harding scandals and gain him four more years in the White House.

	Democrats	Republicans
President:	Alfred E. Smith	Herbert C. Hoover
Vice-President:	Joseph T. Robinson	Charles Curtis

Republican President Calvin Coolidge startled the country with his "I do not choose to run" message. The Democrats picked this up in their sheet music, which was called "Good-bye Cal, Hello Al" in support of Democratic candidate Alfred E. Smith.

The famous songwriter Irving Berlin wrote this song in support of Al Smith for the presidency. Labeled the hit song of the campaign, it was still not popular enough to win the election for the Democrats.

REGULAR DEMOCRATIC NOMINATION

FOR PRESIDENT   FOR VICE-PRESIDENT

HONEST
ABLE
FEARLESS

ALFRED E. SMITH
OF NEW YORK

JOE T. ROBINSON
OF ARKANSAS

The Democratic National Convention of 1928 was held in Houston, Texas, on June 26th to overcome southern hostility to Smith. The "Happy Warrior," as he was dubbed by Franklin D. Roosevelt, won the party nomination. Senator Robinson of Arkansas was the vice-presidential nominee.

This plaque showed Governor Smith, the four-time governor of New York, minus the derby hat that was to become his symbol. Al Smith was a self-made man with a good record in the state of New York, despite the fact that he had come from a Tammany background.

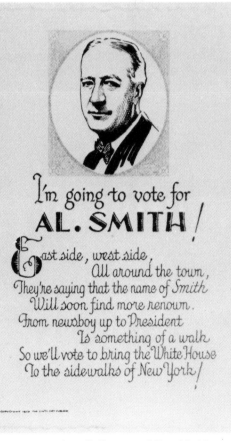

I'm going to vote for AL. SMITH!

East side, west side,
    All around the town,
They're saying that the name of Smith
    Will soon find more renown.
From newsboy up to President
    Is something of a walk
So we'll vote to bring the White House
    To the sidewalks of New York!

This campaign handbill stressed Smith's New York background with the popular song, "East Side, West Side." It was intended to show that Smith had come up the political ladder the hard way — from lowly newsboy to president. Despite the fact that he was a Roman Catholic, opposed to the prohibition law, and a product of Tammany, he was a popular man with eastern Democrats.

Many of the party faithful wore campaign buttons for the "Happy Warrior." But the opposition cries of "Rum, Romanism and Tammany" turned the rural South to the Republican candidate.

Since Franklin Delano Roosevelt nominated Al Smith at the Democratic convention in Houston, it is hardly likely that Smith would have criticized Roosevelt's currency policies. Although the cartoon shown here is a rather mild example, Republican cartoons often carried some of the ugliest mudslinging to be seen in any political campaign.

This very colorful banner for Al Smith hung in many political halls in 1928. The background was purple with a bold yellow border and the red, white, and blue of the flag set off the picture of the candidate.

Press conferences were held daily on campaign trips, and it is possible that the reporters queried Smith about prohibition. He opposed the law, but supported the party plank to make "an honest effort to enforce the Eighteenth Amendment" since it was the law of the land.

Al Smith is shown here as he campaigned all over the United States. He had great difficulty in combating the whispering campaign that went on about him. Many "dry" organizations such as the Women's Christian Temperance Union opposed him, as did the revived Ku Klux Klan.

As far west as Helena, Montana, Al Smith campaigned vigorously. Here he was made an honorary member of an Indian tribe.

The "Happy Warrior" did not win the election on November 6. This may have been a good loss for the Democrats, as a depression was inevitable. With Hoover's victory over Al Smith in 1928, the Great Depression seemed the result of G.O.P. policy rather than the inevitable course of the time and left the way open for a Democratic victory in the next national election.

	Democrats	Republicans
President:	Franklin D. Roosevelt	Herbert C. Hoover
Vice-President:	John N. Garner	Charles Curtis

The Democratic convention, which opened in Chicago on June 27, was deadlocked, with seven candidates in contention. Ultimately, the vote went to F.D.R., the popular governor of New York. Such prominent party men as William G. McAdoo and William Randolph Hearst helped swing the final vote to Roosevelt.

Franklin D. Roosevelt, who was crippled with polio in 1921, broke with tradition by coming to the convention in Chicago and accepting his nomination for president in person. He was the first candidate to do this.

John Nance Garner of Texas became the vice-presidential candidate. The campaign cigar box shown here was typical of the type of campaign material used at this time.

Prominent song and dance man Eddie Cantor supported Franklin Roosevelt. The sheet music shown here was suggested by the famous entertainer and published by Irving Berlin Inc., New York music publishers.

Another popular song of 1932 was "Happy Days Are Here Again." The "Happy Days" bank shown here represented Roosevelt's "new deal" for the American people as well as his commitment to repeal prohibition. This man, who was born with a silver spoon in his mouth, had a winning personality, which inspired confidence in his ability to pull the country out of the Great Depression of '29.

This automobile attachment was also used by party devotees in the 1930s. By this time, the donkey was the acknowledged symbol of the Democratic Party.

This license plate attachment was on many cars in 1932. Roosevelt is shown here as a strong and vigorous young man. He had "charisma," a word that did not come into common use until much later.

Movie star and singer Dick Powell supported Franklin Roosevelt in 1932 with his song, "The Road Is Open Again." The National Recovery Administration, or NRA as it was popularly known, was at the heart of Roosevelt's New Deal program.

Some of the campaign buttons shown here were worn by the party faithful in 1932. By looking at the face of the candidate, you can see how he aged during the time he served as president of the United States.

Ralph E. Becker Collection

Since Roosevelt did win in four presidential elections, it is difficult to date this collection of buttons worn all over the country.

Roosevelt is shown here with Father Charles E. Coughlin, a Roman Catholic priest who was nationally popular at this time. Later, political differences sent the priest and the Protestant in different directions; but in 1932, the men were fighting on the same side.

FIRST the HAM; THEN the HOG!

THE $6,000 HAM

The old postoffice in Uvalde, Tex., which was replaced by a $55,000 one through efforts of Speaker Garner.

THE $55,000 HOG

The new $55,000 postoffice in Uvalde, Tex., home town of Speaker Garner, Democratic vice presidential candidate.

"Postoffice Jack" Garner's billion dollar pork barrel scheme to bring back prosperity by going broke was the culmination of 17 years feeding at the pork barrel trough. As far back as 1915 the Uvalde, Texas, Democrat raided the treasury to build unneeded postoffices in his district.

In a speech at the Atascosa, Texas, fair in that year he said:

"There are a half dozen places in my district where Federal buildings are being erected or have recently been constructed at a cost to the Government far in excess of the actual needs of the communities where they are located.

"Take Uvalde, my own home town, for instance. We are putting up a Post Office down there at a cost of $60,000 when a $5,000 building would be entirely adequate for our needs.... I'll tell you right now *every time one of those Yankees gets a ham, I'm going to do my best to get a hog.*"

A Vote for Garner and Roosevelt is a Vote for More Unneeded Hogs

VOTE FOR HOOVER, CURTIS AND PROSPERITY

Issued by
REPUBLICAN NATIONAL COMMITTEE
Palmer House, Chicago, Ill.

This broadside, issued by the Republican National Committee, was aimed at the Democratic vice-presidential nominee, John Garner of Texas. Garner was accused of excessive spending of federal funds.

During the summer of 1932, veterans assembled in Washington to demonstrate in front of the U.S. Capitol. Known as the Bonus Army, these members of the unemployed were demanding immediate payment of their bonus for wartime service. Aid to the unemployed was one of the gravest problems facing Roosevelt at this time.

The smiles on the faces of the Democratic candidates in this 1932 campaign picture show that they were confident of victory.

	Democrats	Republicans
President:	Franklin D. Roosevelt	Alfred M. Landon
Vice-President:	John N. Garner	Frank Knox

The Democrats decided to stay with Roosevelt at their national convention held in June at the Philadelphia Municipal Auditorium. The repeal of prohibition in 1933 and the beginning of economic stability under the New Deal added to Roosevelt's popularity.

RE-ELECT
VICE-PRESIDENT

JOHN N. GARNER

Once again, John Garner campaigned with F.D.R. as vice-presidential candidate and helped carry the Democratic Party to victory at the polls.

Roosevelt was generally well liked throughout the country. Despite the fact that he was a wealthy man, the people felt he understood their problems and was working to solve them. "Keeping the people's heart in government" meant keeping Roosevelt in office.

This clock, bearing a likeness of Franklin D. Roosevelt superimposed on the U.S. Capitol, was typical of the type of memorabilia being made at this time.

The term "New Deal" on this Roosevelt mug created controversy in 1936. The Republicans regarded the New Deal derogatorily. To the Democrats, however, the New Deal was the solution to the problems left over from the Republican administration and the Depression of '29.

126

PIGS IS PIGS!

THE DOLLAR IN HOG-FARMING

Farmers stood behind Roosevelt in 1936, remembering that he had subsidized them when production had to be cut early in his first term of office to help alleviate the results of the Depression. While they may not have wanted to slaughter Adam Bede's hogs in '36, the farmers still supported F.D.R.

Seated in the car with F.D.R. was his wife, Eleanor, who actively campaigned for her husband. In a day when women's rights were becoming an issue, Mrs. Roosevelt's active public life served as a model for other women to follow.

	Democrats	Republicans
President:	Franklin D. Roosevelt	Wendell L. Willkie
Vice-President:	Henry A. Wallace	Charles L. McNary

Ralph E. Becker Collection

During his first two terms in office, F.D.R. proved himself to be a friend of labor. He pulled the country out of the Depression, and many Americans agreed with his major policies. At a time when war in Europe was frightening Americans, Roosevelt was promising not to send boys to fight on foreign soil. "Roosevelt, Our Next President" was heard throughout the land.

1.   In 1840 the opposition party, which was then known as the Whigs, used the log cabin as a campaign symbol. Harrison campaigned vigorously using log cabins in many parades and on campaign literature. Log cabins were erected throughout the country and used as campaign headquarters.

2.   This Tammany Bank was a popular campaign item in 1872. Boss Tweed of the Tammany Gang supported the Democratic candidate, Horace Greeley, and the opposition made much of the corruption in New York politics.

3. Chester Arthur was only the Republican vice-presidential candidate when this banner was made. Due to the death of President Garfield, he became the twenty-first president of the United States.

4. The Democratic Party won the election of
1884 with the candidates shown on this elegant
campaign banner — Grover Cleveland for
president and Thomas A. Hendricks for vice-
president. The platform of the party hoped for
''prosperity to our common country.''

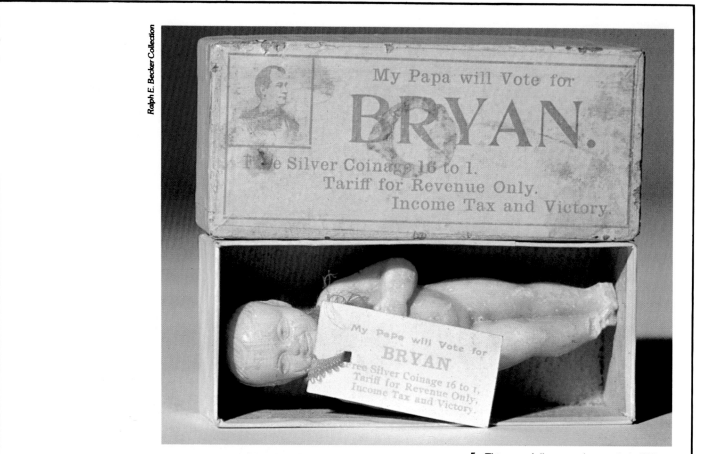

5. This soap doll was made up to help William Jennings Bryan in the campaign of 1896. Unfortunately, the soap did not wash away Republican votes and Bryan lost the election.

6. Bryan was once again in the presidential limelight for the Democrats in 1908. Because he came from Nebraska, he was a favorite with the Midwestern farmers as shown here on this sheet music. However, once again, he was beaten out for the presidency by the Republicans.

d

7. This nutcracker with the Woodrow Wilson head dates to about 1912, the year the New Jersey governor was elected to the presidency.

8. Governor Al Smith was the Democratic candidate for president in 1928. This campaign included some of the ugliest mudslinging ever seen, some of which caused Governor Smith to lose the election to Herbert Hoover.

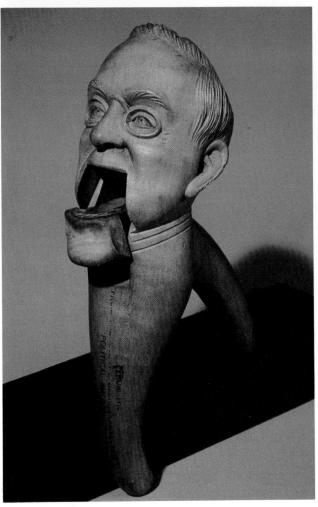

9. "Happy Days Are Here Again" was a song played over and over again on the radio in 1932. It was a catchy campaign song and one that promised the repeal of the generally disliked prohibition law.

10. In 1940, despite a war-torn Europe, the United States was still neutral. Franklin Delano Roosevelt, running for his third term as president, hoped to keep the country out of war. He won the election becoming the first United States president to serve more than two terms.

11. Nineteen forty-eight was the year the Democrats began wooing the women's vote. The sheet music shown here declares that "The Girl I Love is a Democrat."

12. The 1948 Democrats elected the Missouri-born haberdasher who assumed the presidency on the death of Franklin D. Roosevelt. Harry S. Truman was a down-to-earth man who talked in a language that the people understood and grew to love.

13. The tall Texan who became president on the death of John Kennedy is shown here in 1964 seeking votes by pledging to continue Kennedy's programs. Lyndon B. Johnson did win the election and did continue as president for another four years.

14. History might have read differently had an assassin's bullet not killed Bobby Kennedy while he was making an acceptance speech after winning the California Primary. The year was 1968, and Kennedy's death was considered still another tragedy in the long history of tragedies for the Kennedy family.

The Chicago Democratic National Convention began on July 15. Franklin D. Roosevelt won the nomination for the presidency on the first ballot. To appease the isolationists both in the party and in the country, one plank of the Democratic platform was against participation in foreign wars.

F.D.R. now stood for "Freedom, Democracy and Roosevelt" and was featured on this patriotic license plate attachment.

Despite the fact that there had been a no-third-term tradition from the beginning of the country's history, Roosevelt planned to run again. Banners, like this one, told the voters to give him another term.

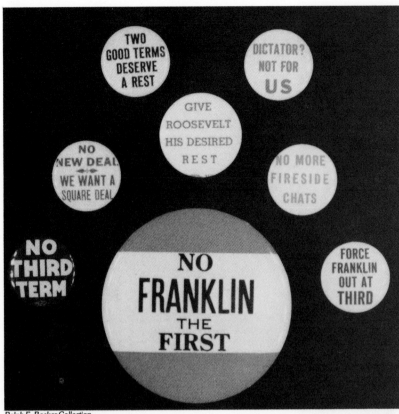

Ralph E. Becker Collection

The cry of dictatorship by Democratic opposition was answered with the slogan — "Don't swap horses in mid-stream." However, political buttons like "No Franklin the First" were widely distributed by the opposition.

Staunch Republican Willkie supporters, as well as members of minor political parties, aimed some of their opposition at Mrs. Roosevelt, a very active participant in politics at this time. Eleanor was warned to start packing her bags and Franklin was told to "Hide at Hyde," his large home in New York State.

Despite the opposition, Mrs. Roosevelt was much in evidence both at the convention and during the campaign itself. Here she is shown being cheered at the Democratic National Convention in Chicago.

Roosevelt and the Democrats quoted George Washington in the debates over the third-term question. The Father of Our Country had stated that a great emergency and a good man were reason enough to keep that good man serving his country. In this poster, the pillars of American democracy were Washington, Wilson, and now Roosevelt.

PILLARS of AMERICAN DEMOCRACY

FOUNDER   INTERPRETER   PROMULGATOR

This collection of Democratic campaign buttons shows the positive thinking of the party during the campaign. Despite the opposition of labor leader John L. Lewis, most labor wanted Roosevelt. Likewise, some of the major newspapers of the day supported F.D.R.

FOR VICE-PRESIDENT

HENRY A. WALLACE

Henry A. Wallace from Iowa was Roosevelt's hand-picked candidate for vice-president. Wallace had served as secretary of agriculture during Roosevelt's second term and was therefore responsible for some of the Democratic farm policies. The combination of urban New Yorker Roosevelt and rural Iowan Wallace defeated the Republican Party and put F.D.R. in the White House for a third term.

	Democrats	Republicans
President:	Franklin D. Roosevelt	Thomas E. Dewey
Vice-President:	Harry S. Truman	John W. Brickers

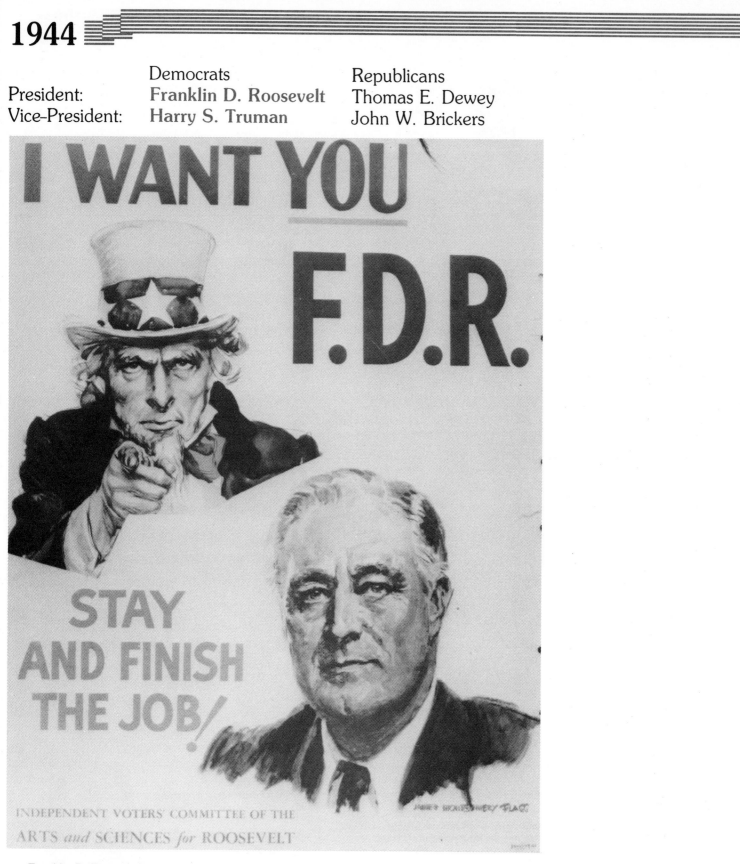

Franklin D. Roosevelt received the presidential nomination at the Democratic National Convention held in Chicago in July 1944. The slogan "Stay and finish the job" shown on this political poster indicated that the Democratic delegates were in favor of a fourth term for this dynamic man.

Roosevelt was now a wartime president. The attack on Pearl Harbor and the declaration of war had taken place in December 1941, and American men were fighting on not one but two fronts. By 1944 the country wanted Roosevelt to lead them to peace, and the large aircraft carrier shown on this pennant symbolized America's winning the war with its Air Force.

1944
CAMPAIGN SONG

— ★ —

LET'S
RE - RE - RE-ELECT
ROOSEVELT

— ★ —

A SNAPPY MARCH TUNE
Words That Mean Something

— ★ —

DEDICATED TO
THE COMMANDER - IN - CHIEF

F.D.R. ran for president on a Democratic platform of supporting the founding of an international organization to prevent aggression in the world. His postwar plans and policies were geared to appeal to veterans, farmers, and labor alike. The song shown on the sheet music here — "Let's Re-Re-Re-Elect Roosevelt" — was heard often during the campaign.

135

Both the broadside and the political button shown here stressed the twelve years of experience that F.D.R. had already had in the presidency. The leadership qualities shown by Roosevelt from 1932 on were in evidence as he guided the country through World War II. The country was afraid of a change and showed it by voting Democratic at the polls.

This phonograph record showed a positive side of Roosevelt's activities while he was president. Rumors of his ill health were dispelled by his public appearances for causes like the March of Dimes.

In the hard-fought political campaign to reelect F.D.R., little attention was paid to his running mate, Harry S. Truman, senator from Missouri. However, with the death of the president at Warm Springs, Georgia, on April 12, 1945, Vice-President Truman was sworn into office as the thirty-third president of the United States.

	Democrats	Republicans
President:	Harry S. Truman	Thomas E. Dewey
Vice-President:	Alben W. Barkley	Earl Warren

Democratic campaign buttons in 1948 were for the feisty Harry S. Truman, who had succeeded to the presidency on the death of Franklin D. Roosevelt. The man from Missouri was outspoken but well liked by the people.

This banner to reelect Truman may have waved at the Democratic National Convention, which began in Philadelphia on July 12.

BEAT HIGH PRICES

ELECT
★ HARRY S. TRUMAN ★
PRESIDENT
★ ALBEN W. BARKLEY ★
VICE-PRESIDENT

The nominees who won at the Democratic National Convention were Harry Truman for president and Alben W. Barkley, senator from the southern state of Kentucky. The choice of Barkley as vice-president was an attempt to gather votes from the strongly Democratic South.

Delegates and party devotees wore Truman neckties in support of their candidate. When Truman campaigned, large crowds turned out to hear him all over the country, despite the fact that the press felt he was doomed to lose the election.

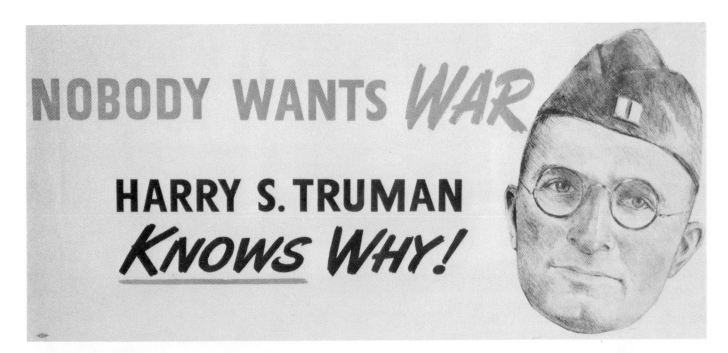

NOBODY WANTS *WAR*

HARRY S. TRUMAN *KNOWS WHY!*

This picture of a military-looking Harry Truman was an attempt to appeal to the veterans he had brought home. The Democratic Party made a strong civil rights statement in its platform, as well as promises to control inflation and to repeal the Taft-Hartley Act.

The limousine in the forefront of this picture carries Harry Truman, his wife, Bess, and his daughter, Margaret. The parade was in front of the Washington Post Building in Washington, D.C.

Whistle-stop campaigning was done by Republican presidential nominee Dewey and his running mate, Earl Warren, as well as by Harry Truman. Truman campaigned vigorously, covering some 31,000 miles. He denounced the Eightieth Congress, blaming it for everything from high prices to the hated Taft-Hartley Act, which attempted to regulate the problems between labor and management.

Reprinted, courtesy of the Chicago Tribune

When Truman went to bed on November 2, he thought he was a beaten man. Even the *Chicago Daily Tribune* prepared its early issues with a headline proclaiming Dewey the winner. Later election returns assured Harry Truman that he was to remain in the White House for another four years.

	Democrats	Republicans
President:	Adlai E. Stevenson	Dwight D. Eisenhower
Vice-President:	John J. Sparkman	Richard M. Nixon

Ralph E. Becker Collection

President Truman announced his decision not to run for reelection in April 1952. This threw the Democratic convention in Chicago into a quandary, with favorite sons appearing from all over the country. One logical candidate was the governor of Illinois, Adlai E. Stevenson. Stevenson was from the Midwest, had a grandfather who had been vice-president under Grover Cleveland, and had a way of successfully handling the opposition in his own home state.

Television cameras were grinding away at the July convention. Somehow, the convention appeared more like a carnival than a serious gathering where the nomination of candidates was the main concern.

Adlai Stevenson was introduced to the convention by President Truman, who had come from Washington for that express purpose. Truman actively supported Stevenson throughout the campaign.

Banners like this one hung at Democratic gatherings all over the country. Vice-presidential candidate John J. Sparkman, the fifty-two year old senator from Alabama, was a liberal despite his opposition to civil rights legislation.

The Democratic donkey is seen here kicking the daylights out of "them" — but unfortunately for the donkey, General Eisenhower was ultimately too popular for the Democrats to defeat.

Both parties used advertising on cigarette packs as a means of reaching the smoking public.

The "It" referred to in this campaign sheet music was the prosperity that the Democrats had given the country since 1932. The farmer and the laborer were both encouraged to support Adlai.

Stevenson buttons were worn prominently wherever the candidate appeared. However, Stevenson had his problems, one of which was the southern vote. Stevenson spoke loud and clear to uphold the party platform plank, which was in favor of new civil rights legislation.

Although the banner stretched across the street reads for Stevenson and Sparkman, the men walking in the parade at the time this picture was taken are Republicans Eisenhower and Dewey. Who had the parade permit that day — the Republicans or the Democrats?

TOO CLOSE FOR COMFORT!

	OHIO	CALIFORNIA
Truman	1,452,791	1,913,134
Dewey	1,445,684	1,895,269
	7,107	17,865

DEPRESSION

MISSED US by only 12,487 Votes. If only 12,487 of 6,957,609 Voters in California and Ohio had switched to Dewey in 1948, Truman would have lost. Five million voters stayed home. Your State may decide this year's election results by a few votes.

Don't Gamble On Poverty with the GOP

STAY SAFE — VOTE STEVENSON

Labor's Committee for Stevenson and Sparkman

GEORGE M. HARRISON, *Chairman*   E. L. OLIVER, *Secretary-Treasurer*
1621 K Street, N.W., Washington 5, D.C.

The Democrats were well aware of how close the election was in 1948. Concerted efforts were made to get out the vote as well as to stress the idea of prosperity with the Democrats or "poverty with the GOP."

IF YOU STAY HOME
on Nov. 4
You *WILL* be voting

FOR
{
Boom, Bust and Breadlines

Wage Slashes

Higher Rents

Tougher anti-labor laws
}

VOTE FOR CONTINUED PROSPERITY
VOTE STEVENSON
Labor's Committee for Stevenson and Sparkman

GEORGE M. HARRISON, *Chairman*   E. L. OLIVER, *Secretary-Treasurer*
1621 K Street, N.W., Washington 5, D.C.

November 4, 1952, was election day, and despite broadsides like this, Stevenson and Sparkman lost.

	Democrats	Republicans
President:	Adlai E. Stevenson	Dwight D. Eisenhower
Vice–President:	Estes Kefauver	Richard M. Nixon

The Democratic National Convention began in Chicago on August 13, later than earlier campaigns because television and air travel reduced the time needed for campaigning. The Old Guard was divided as Truman supported Harriman of New York while Eleanor Roosevelt gave her support to Stevenson. Adlai Stevenson won the nomination for president.

Estes Kefauver, senator from Tennessee, won the vice-presidential nomination against such opposition as Hubert Humphrey of Minnesota, John Kennedy of Massachussetts, Albert Gore of Tennessee, and Robert Wagner of New York. During the campaign that followed, Kefauver concentrated his efforts in the Midwest, where he had always been a popular figure.

The Stevenson camp claimed support from the GOP, but this was actually wishful thinking. The country at large was happy with "Ike."

WE'VE HAD IT!

WE'RE GOING DEMOCRATIC

TO STEVENSON CAMP

COURTESY OF NORMAN IMPELMAN, S.F. CALIF.

As the poster says, Stevenson was "pledged to action on school construction and child welfare." However, there was also a civil rights plank in the party platform. This plank, while opposed to discrimination, only promised not to use force to implement the recent decision of the Supreme Court.

Adlai Stevenson was caught one day at a Labor Day Rally in Flint, Michigan, wearing a shoe with a hole in the sole. The picture of this was widely circulated and used by both parties. The Democrats hailed Stevenson as a man of the people, who even managed to get holes in his shoes.

The small print on this game reads — "This game is especially rigged so a Republican can't win." However, even games like this could not bring victory to the Democrats. The country was lethargic politically, and was satisfied that Ike had ended the Korean War and that there was little inflation. Although the Republicans took the White House again, the Congress elected was Democratic.

	Democrats	Republicans
President:	John F. Kennedy	Richard M. Nixon
Vice-President:	Lyndon B. Johnson	Henry C. Lodge

THE NEW YORK TIMES, SUNDAY, APRIL 24, 1960.   E 3

THE PRESIDENTIAL RACE—COMMENTS ON THE CANDIDATES IN BOTH PARTIES

Ralph E. Becker Collection

Presidential hopefuls abounded this election year as shown in this *New York Times* cartoon. Even Adlai Stevenson was considered as a possible candidate. The young John Kennedy, Hubert Humphrey, Stuart Symington, and Lyndon Johnson were all possibilities.

Los Angeles was the scene of the Democratic National Convention, and the delegates assembled there on July 11. This picture of Kennedy headquarters in Los Angeles shows the excitement that prevailed before and during the convention.

PRESIDENT
of the
UNITED STATES

Ralph E. Becker Collection

John F. Kennedy was the senator from Massachussetts, whom some declared was too young for the presidency. At forty-three years of age, he came on the national political scene as a rich man's son, a graduate of Harvard University, and a man with an exceptional record as a hero in World War II. His personality as well as his good looks helped to win him the Democratic nomination. The Democrats saw in him a new promise for America — someone who would lead the so-called "New Frontier."

Kennedy, "The Best Man," stood strongly for the civil rights plank in the party platform. This plank called for federal action if needed to give all the citizens the right to vote and equality in all phases of American life.

Those who wore this Kennedy hat saw their candidate take the party nomination on the very first ballot.

Vests, like this campaign vest, gave a youthful lift to campaigning. John F. Kennedy, with his attractive young wife and little girl, may have been part of a rich man's society, but he had personal appeal.

Ralph E. Becker Collection

Campaign cigars were used for Nixon and Kennedy in 1960. Tobacco and tobacco products have been used to support candidates as far back as the mid-nineteenth century.

Lyndon Johnson, Democratic nominee for vice–president, was the strongest southern Democratic candidate since the Civil War. He had served as Democratic majority leader of the Senate, and he campaigned vigorously for himself and Kennedy during the campaign of 1960.

KENNEDY-JOHNSON

two great Democrats

This poster of smiling candidates was widely circulated during the 1960 presidential campaign. Kennedy traveled many miles in his personal airplane and Johnson made whistle-stops all over the South in his train, the *L.B.J. Victory Special.*

WINNER TAKES ALL!

**IN THIS RACE—
NO SECOND PLACE!**

For Full Speed Over Those Hurdles
Vote **x** KENNEDY FOR PRESIDENT

Labor's Committee for Kennedy & Johnson, 1801 K Street, N.W., Washington 6, D.C.
Geo. M. Harrison, Chairman   E. L. Oliver, Secretary-Treasurer

National campaign issues shown in this broadside include education, economic growth, and military strength. It also shows that world leadership would go to the United States rather than to the communists if Kennedy were elected.

Crowds surrounded John Kennedy's car as he stopped to speak to the people. Shown seated beside him is his wife, Jacqueline, who was expecting their second child at this time. For this reason, Jackie was not able to be more active in the campaign. The public loved this very human side of their candidate.

This campaign dinner plate showed the popular young couple who were to become residents at 1600 Pennsylvania Avenue. Although the popular vote was very close in this presidential ballot, Jack Kennedy won the day.

The headline tells the tragic story that rocked the entire country. John Kennedy was assassinated in Dallas on November 22, 1963. Lyndon Johnson, the tall man from Texas, was sworn in as the thirty-sixth president of the United States aboard *Air Force One,* the presidential plane.

1964

	Democrats	Republicans
President:	Lyndon B. Johnson	Barry M. Goldwater
Vice-President:	Hubert H. Humphrey	William E. Miller

DEMOCRATS CONVENE IN ATLANTIC CITY
AUGUST 24

The Democratic Convention will open August 24 in Atlantic City, New Jersey. In all probability, the delegates will renominate President Lyndon B. Johnson by acclamation.

But a handful of unsettled problems will lend drama and suspense to the meeting. The greatest excitement will probably center arond the task of selecting a candidate for Vice President.

This will be the first time in its history as a convention mecca that Atlantic City will be the site of a national political convention. The immense Convention Hall, the largest building of its kind in the world, plays host each year to more giant gatherings than any other in the nation. Horse shows, football games, auto races, Miss America contests, and even polo games have drawn large crowds to the hall. During World War II, it was a training center for more than 500,000 men.

The huge structure covers seven acres. Its main auditorium, 537 feet long and 288 feet wide, seats 41,000. Its stage, also the world's largest, can be fitted with seats for 2,000 more. The ballroom, the conference and committee rooms, with a total seating capacity of 17,000, will provide space for the party headquarters. One thousand cars can park in the garage under the main floor. A pipe organ in the hall is the world's largest, with 32,913 pipes.

The city itself has more than 30,000 hotel and motel rooms to house the delegates. Another 6,000 rooms are available within the surrounding suburban communities.

When the delegates can snatch a moment from their duties, they will find many facilities for relaxation. Theatres, night clubs, fine restaurants, and some of the best beaches and swimming areas on the east coast will offer a respite from the tense, grueling hours in the caucus rooms and Convention Hall.

"In all probability, the delegates will renominate President Lyndon B. Johnson by acclamation." This sentence, included in a write-up of the coming Democratic National Convention in Atlantic City, proved to be true. It is interesting to note that the skyline of Atlantic City shown here has altered considerably since that time.

ALL THE WAY...WITH L. B. J.

Title by DR. HERMAN SILVERS

Lyrics by ELI L. SCHAFF
Music by BEE WALKER

As sung by
LAURA LANE
during the
Democratic Convention
in Atlantic City, N.J.
1964

Published by
ZUMA MUSIC CO.
200 West 54th Street
New York, N.Y. 10019

President Johnson had had experience in uniting dissenting factions when he was a senator on Capitol Hill. The song "All the way . . . with L.B.J." was sung at the convention in Atlantic City.

Automobile attachments, like the one shown here, were widely circulated during and after the convention.

1964 Democratic National Convention Issue

HELLO

LYNDON

ED AMES WITH THE "HELLO, DOLLY!" MALE CHORUS

Based on the hit song, "Hello, Dolly!" by Jerry Herman. From the Broadway show, "Hello, Dolly!"

The popular Broadway tune "Hello Dolly" provided a theme song for the Democrats. "Hello Lyndon" was heard on radio and television constantly. The actor-singer Ed Ames helped to popularize this catchy political song.

THE ART PRESS INC., CHICAGO

COPYRIGHT 1964, DEMOCRATIC NATIONAL COMMITTEE

President Johnson chose Senator Hubert Humphrey as his running mate for 1964. This well-known Midwestern liberal was an excellent speaker with a winning personality. His campaigning style complemented that of President Johnson, and helped take them both back to Washington.

Handkerchief bandannas such as this one showed President Johnson and his First Lady, Lady Bird. Mrs. Johnson was an asset to her husband both during and after the campaign; her beautification project left a lasting impression on the nation.

This collection of campaign buttons shows various women from both parties through the years.

President Johnson won the 1964 campaign for the White House with his plans for the "Great Society." This phrase was supposed to be synonymous with (as yet unaccomplished) peace and prosperity. Here, Mr. Johnson is signing into law the 1964 Civil Rights Act. Among the prominent people watching this important signing were Lady Bird, Senator Robert Kennedy, Vice-President Humphrey, and Martin Luther King. Others seated here in the East Room of the White House were congressional and civil rights leaders.

	Democrats	Republicans
President:	Hubert Humphrey	Richard M. Nixon
Vice President:	Edmund S. Muskie	Spiro T. Agnew

The Democratic delegates assembled at Chicago in 1968 did not know what was happening outside the amphitheater but millions of television viewers all over the country did. Mayor Daley's "Gestapo tactics" against demonstrators were called "tragic events of the week" by a troubled but victorious candidate, Hubert H. Humphrey.

Humphrey hoped to reunite his party, which had placed such names in nomination for primary elections as Eugene McCarthy and Robert Kennedy. Kennedy's assassination at the California primary was also seen by millions of television viewers.

Senator Edmund S. Muskie of Maine became Humphrey's running mate, and his name appears on this Humphrey donkey bank, popular during the campaign.

UNITE WITH HUMPHREY

Hubert Humphrey had worked in a pharmacy as a young man, and so his followers called his party headquarters in Washington "The Pharmacy." His liberal views and unassuming background were what the party hoped would bring him victory.

The racial violence that followed the assassination of Martin Luther King in 1967 continued into the campaign of 1968. Most of the walkers in the Poor People's Campaign were black and asking the government for more protection in the way of civil rights.

Vietnam, that "unpopular war," was perhaps the worst problem of the campaign of 1968. President Johnson's declaration to end the bombing came shortly before the election. It was too little and too late by that time to help Humphrey win. The Republicans took over the country with Nixon and Agnew.

	Democrats	Republicans
President:	George McGovern	**Richard M. Nixon**
Vice-President:	R. Sargent Shriver	**Spiro T. Agnew**

Senator George McGovern of South Dakota won the presidential nomination at the Democratic National Convention in Miami Beach in July. The vice-presidential slot went to Missouri Senator Thomas F. Eagleton, McGovern's choice for the office. However, after the convention had adjourned, Senator Eagleton withdrew from the national ticket for personal reasons. R. Sargent Shriver of Maryland then became the vice-presidential candidate on the Democratic ticket.

McGovern was a popular candidate because of his strong views on the Vietnam War. The platform and the candidate pledged "immediate and complete withdrawal of all U.S. forces in Indochina."

This political button from 1972 showing McGovern and Shriver stressed the idea that the Democrats would bring the troops home from abroad. Although McGovern promised to end military aid to Saigon, he also pledged to help Vietnam economically recover from the war.

Because the twenty-sixth amendment to the Constitution had been passed in 1971, eighteen, nineteen, and twenty year olds had the right to vote for the first time in a national election. Young voters were wooed with such campaign items as this scarf.

© 1971 by McQ. Inc

The crying eagle shown on this poster symbolized the American system in times that were troubled by Vietnam, repression, and racial prejudice.

The items shown here symbolize the needs of the young people of 1972. The crying eagle and emerging butterfly were well-known symbols of an emerging voting force in the United States.

The denim shoulder and tote bags were carried by many young people, who were going to vote for the first time in this national election.

The unrest on college campuses and elsewhere is reflected in these anti-war buttons. Even the quote from Vice-President Agnew about being an "effete snob" was directed toward desires for peace.

This collection of anti-war and anti-Nixon campaign buttons reflects the feeling against the Republicans in the early 1970s.

In the early 1970s, this banner was used in demonstrations for peace; later it was used for impeachment of President Nixon. The fight was on for changes in both domestic and foreign policies.

Because of political corruption, both of the 1968 Republican candidates resigned from office — Agnew due to corruption charges in his own state of Maryland and Nixon because of the Watergate scandal. The break-in of Democratic headquarters by Republicans and the ensuing cover-up provided many hours of listening to incriminating tapes. Here, Judge Sirica and defendants Mitchell, Haldeman, and Ehrlichman are listening to the tapes. This drawing is by Freda Reiter.

	Democrats	Republicans
President:	Jimmy Carter	Gerald R. Ford
Vice-President:	Walter Mondale	Robert Dole

The Democrats met for their National Convention in New York City in July. Lamp post signs like the one shown here decorated the street outside of Convention Hall to welcome the delegates attending.

This paper place mat was used inside the convention to celebrate the country's Bicentennial year. Smiling Jimmy Carter, ex-governor of Georgia, won the nomination for president on the first ballot. He had announced his candidacy in 1974 and had done a lot of campaigning to get his name known across the country.

1776 ★ THE UNITED STATES of AMERICA BICENTENNIAL CELEBRATION ★ 1976

New York City site of the
'76 DEMOCRATIC
NATIONAL CONVENTION

Signing the Declaration of Independence

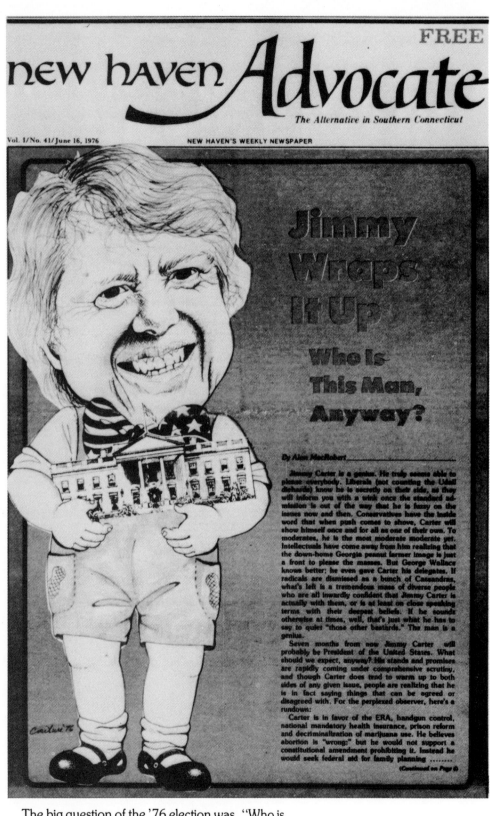

FREE

new haven Advocate

The Alternative in Southern Connecticut

Vol. 1/No. 41/June 16, 1976   NEW HAVEN'S WEEKLY NEWSPAPER

Jimmy Wraps It Up

Who Is This Man, Anyway?

By Alan MacRobert

Jimmy Carter is a genius. He truly seems able to please everybody. Liberals (not counting the Udall diehards) know he is secretly on their side, as they will inform you with a wink once the standard admission "is out of the way that he is fuzzy on the issues now and then. Conservatives have the inside word that when push comes to shove, Carter will show himself once and for all as one of their own. To moderates, he is the most moderate moderate yet. Intellectuals have come away from him realizing that the down-home Georgia peanut farmer image is just a front to please the masses. But George Wallace knows better; he even gave Carter his delegates. If radicals are dismissed as a bunch of Cassandras, what's left is a tremendous mass of diverse people who are all inwardly confident that Jimmy Carter is actually with them, or is at least on close speaking terms with their deepest beliefs. If he sounds otherwise at times, well, that's just what he has to say to quiet "those other bastards." The man is a genius.

Seven months from now Jimmy Carter will probably be President of the United States. What should we expect, anyway? His stands and promises are rapidly coming under comprehensive scrutiny, and though Carter does tend to warm up to both sides of any given issue, people are realizing that he is in fact saying things that can be agreed or disagreed with. For the perplexed observer, here's a rundown:

Carter is in favor of the ERA, handgun control, national mandatory health insurance, prison reform and decriminalization of marijuana use. He believes abortion is "wrong," but he would not support a constitutional amendment prohibiting it. Instead he would seek federal aid for family planning ....

(Continued on Page 6)

The big question of the '76 election was, "Who is this man Jimmy Carter?" Jimmy Carter was a peanut farmer, an engineer, and a man with liberal ideas on racial issues. He had stood up for his belief in racial equality in his home state of Georgia, as well as throughout the nation while campaigning.

Senator Walter Mondale of Minnesota took the second spot on the Democratic ticket, bringing western support to Carter.

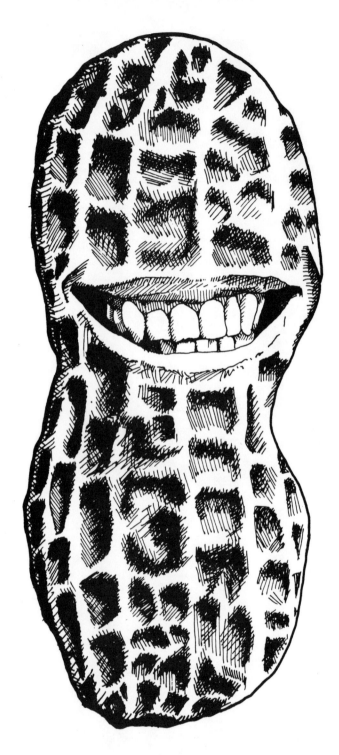

Carter for President

Although an entire nation had been eating peanuts for generations, when the peanut farmer ran for president the peanut became a campaign symbol.

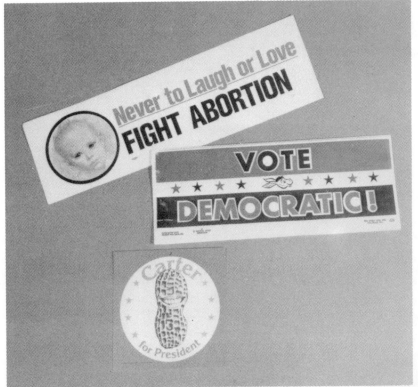

Stickers for the presidential campaign were used to present the candidate's name, to encourage a large voter turnout, and to fight the controversial issue of abortion.

Four television debates were held by the major candidates for the nation to witness. Here, Carter and Ford are making notes prior to the start of one of the debates.

Plains, Georgia, had been an unknown small
town before Jimmy Carter ran for president. As the
hometown of the Democratic candidate, Plains
became a large spot on the map. Here, Carter is
shown speaking from Plains.

Straw hats were worn for both candidates in the
presidential election of 1976.

This collection of over 100 political campaign buttons shows the many men and women who aspired to the White House from both leading parties.

More political buttons, including one showing Carter's teeth, were seen all over the country. This kind of enthusiasm undoubtedly helped win the election for the Democrats and put Jimmy Carter in office as president of the United States.

Bibliography

Binkley, Wilfred E. *American Political Parties*. New York: Alfred A. Knopf, 1963.

Brogan, D.W. *Politics in America*. New York: Harper and Brothers, 1954.

Buchanan, Lamont. *Ballot for Americans*. New York: E. P. Dutton, 1956.

Chambers, William Nisbet and Burnham, Walter Dean. *The American Party Systems*. New York: Oxford University Press, 1975.

Clements, John. *Chronology of the United States*. McGraw Hill, Inc., 1975.

Congressional Quarterly, Inc. *Elections '76*. Washington, D.C.: Congressional Quarterly, 1976.

Congressional Quarterly, Inc. *National Party Conventions 1831-1972*. Washington, D.C.: Congressional Quarterly, 1976.

Durant, John and Alice. *Pictorial History of American Presidents*. A. S. Barnes & Co., 1955.

Felknor, Bruce L. *Dirty Politics*. New York: W. W. Norton & Company, Inc., 1966.

Goodman, William. *The Two-Party System in the United States*. New York: D. Van Nostrand Company, Inc., 1964.

Harsch, Joseph C. *The Role of Political Parties U.S.A.* Washington, D.C.: League of Women Voters Education Fund, 1955.

Hess, Stephen and Kaplan, Milton. *The Ungentlemanly Art*. New York: Macmillan Publishing Co., 1975.

Hoff, Syd. *Editorial and Political Cartooning*. New York: Stravon Educational Press, 1976.

Hofstadter, Richard, Miller, William and Aaron, Daniel. *The United States, The History of a Republic*. New Jersey: Prentice-Hall, Inc., 1967.

Kahler, James G. *Hail to the Chief*. Princeton: Pyne Press, 1972.

Kane, Joseph Nathan. *Facts About the Presidents*. New York: H. W. Wilson Company, 1974.

Murphy, Paul L. *Political Parties in American History*. Vol. 3. New York: G. P. Putnam Sons, 1974.

Porter, Kirk H. and Johnson, Donald Bruce. *National Party Platforms 1840-1964*. Urbana and London: University of Illinois Press, 1966.

Roseboom, Eugene H. *A History of Presidential Elections*. New York: Macmillan Company, 1970.

Silber, Irwin. *Songs America Voted By*. Pennsylvania: Stackpole Books, 1971.

Taylor, Tim. *The Book of Presidents*. New York: Arno Press, 1972.

Vinson, J. Chal. *Thomas Nast, Political Cartoonist*. Athens, Georgia: University of Georgia Press, 1967.

Williams, T. Harry, Current, Richard M. and Friedel, Frank. *History of the United States Since 1865*. New York: Alfred A. Knopf, 1961.

Index